The
Practice Of
Nigerian
Federalism

The
Practice Of
Nigerian
Federalism

Sunday C. Enubuzor, Ph.D.

To order additional copies of this book, contact:
Xlibris Corporation
1-888-795-4274
www.Xlibris.com
Orders@Xlibris.com
113526

CONTENTS

Acknowledgment

I am grateful to my beloved wife, Dr. Harriet L. Enubuzor, MD., and children, Chukwuma, Ekeze, Emeka, Christine, and Catherine Enubuzor. They have given me the optimum support and encouragement throughout this process. Their wisdom to challenge me in examining the practice and polity of the Nigerian democratic system of government initiated the writing of this book. They are the love of my life and I am so grateful.

Approaches of Sovereign Democratic Systems of Government

To define the significance of governing, it is important to understand the categories in which systems of governments are classified.

Unitary Approach:

A system of government based on the central government in control of the sovereignty of the entire country. In a unitary government, the central government possesses much authority and decision-making power. Local governing authorities serve as administrative arms of the central government. A unitary government is one in which there is only one level of government that has constitutionally mandated powers. For instance, a nation with a unitary government might have a national government which grants powers to its states, but it has the ability to take away these powers as it wishes. The states have no inherent power granted by the constitution. Also, counties have powers granted to them by the state, which the state can take away. Counties have no inherent, mandated powers in the constitution, unlike states or the national government. A few examples of nations that practiced a Unitary System of government are: The United Kingdom, France, Poland, and Spain. It is important, however, to note that unitary governments are not inherently less Democratic than other forms of government.

Unitary systems are most distinguished from other system of governmental approaches because the possession of power is focus solely on the central government authority. Thus, the central government directly exercises its authority over the citizenry, and may choose to delegate responsibility for certain policy areas or activities to the states or local governmental authorities. The state and local authorities only have those powers which the central government chooses to grant. The central government may alter or abolish state or local authorities at will.

Policies decisions formulated by state or local governments maybe overturned by the central government since the states or local governments do not have exclusive governing powers, delegated powers, and responsibilities. After all, the functions of the state and local government authorities are specified only in statutes and tend to be more administrative, than legislative in nature. States and Local powers are not constitutional entrenched; rather, they are brought into existence through statutes passed by the central government. Thus, this system of organizing government authority will primarily benefit a clear, hierarchical authority structure which eliminates stalemates among the state political units. Furthermore, the embodiment of supreme authority in a single, national government encourages citizens to identify with the country as a whole, rather than expressing divided loyalties to state and local authorities. This distinguishes a unitary system from the federalism government in which the federation's constituents have a mandatory attributes to their sovereign states and rights that the central government must respect.

It is impressing to state that the unitary system is the world's most common form of government that are practiced within the wide spectrum of both democratic and nondemocratic countries. Furthermore the decision-making body of the central government controls all aspects of governance, because there are no powers or functions legally reserved to either the state or local authorities. All areas of government ultimately are under the authority of a single body, so states with unitary systems often have more uniform laws and regulations than federations. The central government also might be responsible for appointing the personnel of state or local level of government. Government decisions in unitary states are not necessarily made by the central authority.

Some additional features of a unitary system include the following:

- States are not permitted to secede from the central government or union government.
- State cannot pass any legislation that is contradictory to public policy or the laws of the central government.
- In a debate about a particular policy of state, being eclipsed by the central government, the judicial system's intervention shall prove to be final.
- Laws made by legislative assembly of the state are restricted to the jurisdiction of the state.
- Laws made by legislation by the central government are applicable to all states.

Pros of Unitary System:

In unitary system, States are statued to simplify and implement effective policies; however, there are some pros and cons that have been observed in the system.

The Pros of Unitary System are enlisted as follows:

- *Efficient Regional Administration*: One of the best features of a unitary system is that the policies that are made by the central government are positively viewed and effectively implemented by the people of the state government. Such implementation reduces the workload of the central government.
- *Respect for Common Law*: One of the greatest demerits of the federal form of government that is overcome by the central government is the respect for common law that has been set by the central government. This makes the legal system transparent.

Cons of the Unitary System:

- *Slow implementation of national policies*: There are several different policies that are to be implemented by the state government, but are prepared and formulated by the central government. Implementation of these policies is quite difficult and time-consuming.
- *New Laws*: Passing new laws and legislation is difficult and deep study has to be done by legislators in order to determine whether the new law is contradictory to the current laws or central government or state government.
- *Regionalism*: One of the imminent risks of a unitary system is the social phenomenon of regionalism. Often such regionalism results into friction between two states.

Confederate Approach:

Is a system of government whereby powers are distributed between State and Local Governments? State and Local Governments protect and preserve their own authorities by forming a weak Central Government. The power of the federal government is split between a Central Government authority and its constituent States. Usually, an overriding law of the land, known as a constitution, allocates duties, rights, and privileges to each level of government. The constitution usually defines how power is shared between national, state, and local governments.

The power to amend this constitution is usually granted to the citizens through their governmental representatives. In principle, the states in a confederation would not lose their separate identity through confederation, and would retain the right of secession. In practice, this right might be difficult to exercise, and the constituent units of a long-standing confederation might appear to be little different from those of any other federal state.

In a confederate system, power is extremely diffuse—there is little central political control. State Government can set fiscal and trade policy (e.g., set tariffs and taxes) and the like. The States might adopt a common currency in a confederation to ease interstate trade. In a confederacy (or confederation), the role of a Central Government is primarily one of foreign policy, providing a collective front to increase the bargaining power of the states. For example, Lagos State by itself might not be able to get a beneficial trade agreement with United Kingdom, but working in concert with the other states, it can get a better deal, since the confederation as a whole is a larger player. The confederate governments can affect some aspects of internal policy as it relates to trade between the states, and other areas of interstate interaction. The bulk of power is devolved—that is, the legislature of any one state can set its own laws independently of any other state like the Sharia laws in most northern states of Nigeria. Also, the states collectively decide national policy. Germany was a confederation before it adopted a federal system (many nations undergo this transformation.)

However, in a federal system, the Central (or Federal) Government has much more authority than in a confederate system. The central government controls more than trade policy, and makes decisions about policy areas that involve interactions between states (such as highway systems). It usually has the power to tax independently of the states and to control the money supply. A Federal Government also usually has its own mechanisms for enforcement. For example, in Nigeria the SSS and the EFCC are the primary agencies for investigating federal crimes and crimes that occur between or among multiple states.

States (or provinces or regions) still set a great deal of policy and law on their own in federal systems, but these policy areas are somewhat more restricted, and the Central Government has its own areas of policy in which States cannot intrude. In a Federal System, federal laws usually trump State laws when the two are in conflict. Thus, some areas of policy are under the sole control of the federal government, some areas are under the control of state governments (state transportation, health/welfare services, criminal law), and some areas overlap. In the federal system of Nigeria, a state can give its citizens more rights than are guaranteed by the constitution, but it can never give fewer rights than the constitution promise.

Federal Systems (or Federations) are more common than Confederation Governments. A Confederation sets up the minimum limits of a nation-state:

it defines a border, it sets rules for passage through the territory within that border, and it sets foreign policy of treaties, war, and peace. A Federal System expands on giving the Central Government more power to regulate internal affairs across state boundaries, and setting minimum guidelines for how government should operate within and among the States.

Totalitarian Approach:

Is a system of government that is predominantly practiced by a monarch; whereby, the power of rulers is not limited by elections. Totalitarian systems also restrict personal freedom in most cases. This is in opposition to a federalist style, in which both States and the Central Government has inherent powers granted by the constitution. It is also a form of government that subordinates all aspects of its citizens' lives to the authority of the central government authority, with a single charismatic leader as the ultimate head. The pursuit of the central authority's goal is the only ideological foundation for such a government. Although the term, totalitarianism was originally intended to designate fascist and communist regimes. The notion of "Totalitarianism" a "total" political power by State was formulated in 1923 by Giovanni Amendola who described Italian Fascism as a system fundamentally different from conventional dictatorship. The term was later assigned a positive meaning in the writings of Giovanni Gentile, Italy's most prominent philosopher and leading theorist of fascism. He used the term "totalitario" to provide the "total representation of the nation and total guidance of national goals." He also described totalitarianism as a society in which the ideology of the State had influences and power over her citizens.

The difference between Authoritarian and Totalitarian Regime:

An Authoritarian regime denotes a state in which the single power holder, that is, an individual dictator, junta, or a committee or small group of political elite—monopolizes political power. Thus, a totalitarian regime attempts to control virtually all aspects of the socioeconomic life including education, art, science, private life and morals of citizens. The authoritarian ideology penetrates into the deepest reaches of societal structure and the totalitarian government seeks to completely control the thoughts and actions of its citizens. The leader(s) of an authoritarian regime is highly corrupt with no ideology and charisma in leadership.

Totalitarian regime denotes a State whereby citizens are totally subject to a governing authority in all aspects of their lives. Political scientists generally see totalitarianism as the extreme form of dictatorship or typical Police State that involves constant indoctrination achieved by propaganda to erase any potential for dissent by anyone. A totalitarian leader is highly charismatic with a legitimize function to rule or govern based on an ideology. Totalitarian regimes maintain themselves in power through secret police, propaganda disseminated through the media, the elimination of open criticism of the regime, and use of terror tactics. Internal and external threats are created to foster unity through fear.

Compared to totalitarian systems, authoritarian systems may also leave a larger sphere for private life, lack a guiding ideology, tolerate some pluralism in social organization, lack the power to mobilize the whole population in pursuit of national goals, and exercise their power within relatively predictable limits. Totalitarian regimes almost uniformly come into being as a result of a revolution which replaces what is generally regarded as an ineffective government. It has been argued that totalitarianism requires a cult of personality around a charismatic leader who is often glorified a "great leader." However, the relationship between totalitarianism and authoritarianism also remains controversial. Some political historian sees totalitarianism as an extreme form of authoritarianism, while others argue that they differ completely. In a totalitarian system, the ruling ideology requires that every aspect of an individual's life become subordinated to the State, including occupation, income, and religion. Personal survival links to the regime's survival, and thus the concepts of "The State" and "The People" become merged.

One can reasonably argue that all totalitarian systems do seem to necessarily require the presence of a living human absolute leader at all times and do expect a certain type of guidance for nearly every aspect of life from that leader. Regardless of whether or not a newly installed leader of a totalitarian regime may happen to possess a certain natural charisma or not, the totalitarian system seems to tend to attempt to systematically impose her charisma onto the leader.

Critics of the concept of totalitarianism often argue that there is no clear distinction between totalitarian and authoritarian regimes, and that such a distinction is only artificially created by those who wish to make certain dictatorships appear better than others, or those who wish to justify their alliance with (or support of) certain dictators rather than others.

Democratic Socialism Approach:

This is a broad political approach that propagates the ideals of socialism within a democratic philosophy that encompasses the doctrine of parliamentary legislative system. The term Democratic Socialism approach fully supports the ideas of a Socialist System. When practiced in a capitalistic framework, its intent is to reform capitalism from within or through a revolutionary transformation. The approach is more centrist in its ideology and equivocally supports the principles of capitalistic system. However, the democratic socialists main approach is to formulate a more equitable and humane society which are referred by some as a welfare state. The other approach that has the same idea of a welfare state and consistent in a capitalistic ideology is the **Social Democracy.** The social democrats are also willing to consider other methods of delivering aides to the poorest of the poor in society. The democratic socialism, on the other hand, are totally committed to planned economy that focuses solely on re-distribution of wealth and power and social ownership of industries. The democratic socialism defends the essential roles of public sectors, particularly regarding healthcare, mass transit, education, unions, and utilities. The approach focuses on mixed economy that protects workers right and consumer cooperatives, and small businesses. Even-though, the democratic socialists' ideologies are in contradiction to real capitalistic state, their approach is conceived to share the characteristics of being both anti-capitalist and anti-authoritarianism.

A social philosopher, Axel Honneth asserted that political and economic ideologies have a social basis which originated from inter-subjective communication between members of society. Honneth argued that individual liberty and private property evolved from a specific social discourse on human activity; hence, humans depends each other in form of social collectivism to achieve a common goal.

Federalism Approach:

Federalism is a system based on democratic rules and institutions in which the power to govern is shared between national and state governments. In case of Nigeria, the founding fathers adopted federalism in the London Constitutional Conference of 1953 because of its fit to Nigerian diversity and demography. Federalism, and all it stands for, underpins powers of the central government shared with the institutions of the State government. The term federalism also depicts a system of government which sovereignty is constitutionally divided between a Central Government and constituents of State Government.

On many occasions, the Supreme Court has been called on to adjudicate what federalism means when there a contradiction in the interpretation of the constitution. However, the Constitution put a great deal of faith in federalism when the Founding Fathers and the British Colonialists first constructed it. Thus, Federalism can be described as a system of government in which a written constitution divides power between a Central Government and regional or sub-divisional governments. Both types of government have official representatives that act directly as serviette of the people that elected them in government. The term "Federal Government" is usually understood to refer exclusively to the National Government based in Abuja. However, this is not an accurate interpretation of the term as it excludes the role played by other aspects of government concerned with the federalist structure.

Federalism can be seen as a compromise between the extreme concentration of power and a loose confederation of independent States for governing a variety of people. Federalism has the virtue of retaining local pride, traditions, and power while allowing the Central Government to handle common problems. The basic principle of Nigerian Federalism is fixed in Chapter 1, Part 1, and General Provision to the Constitution which states:

"We the people of the Federal Republic of Nigeria having firmly and solemnly resolve, to live in unity and harmony as one indivisible and indissoluble sovereign nation under God, dedicated to the promotion of inter-African solidarity, world peace, international co-operation and understanding and to provide for a Constitution for the purpose of promoting the good government and welfare of all persons in our country, on the principles of freedom, equality and justice, and for the purpose of consolidating the unity of our people do hereby make, enact and give to ourselves the following Constitution:" and

"Nigeria shall be a Federation consisting of States and a Federal Capital Territory. There shall be 36 states in Nigeria, that is to say, Abia, Adamawa, Akwa Ibom, Anambra, Bauchi, Bayelsa, Benue, Borno, Cross River, Delta, Ebonyi, Edo, Ekiti, Enugu, Gombe, Imo, Jigawa, Kaduna, Kano, Katsina, Kebbi, Kogi, Kwara, Lagos, Nasarawa, Niger, Ogun, Ondo, Osun, Oyo, Plateau, Rivers, Sokoto, Taraba, Yobe and Zamfara." and

"Each state of Nigeria, named in the first column of Part I of the First Schedule to this Constitution, shall consist of the area shown opposite thereto in the second column of that Schedule. The headquarters of the Governor of each State shall be known as the Capital City of that State as shown in the third column of the said Part I of the First Schedule opposite the State named in the first column thereof.

The Federal Capital Territory, Abuja, shall be as defined in Part II of the First Scheduled to this Constitution. The provisions of

this Constitution in Part I of Chapter VIII hereof shall in relation
to the Federal Capital Territory, Abuja, have effect in the manner
set out there under. There shall be 768 Local Government Areas
in Nigeria as shown in the second column of Part I of the First
Schedule to this Constitution and six area councils as shown in
Part II of that Schedule."

Nigeria has throughout her history practiced horizontal and vertical
federalism. These two patterns of practice are best described below:

Horizontal Federalism:

It is regarded as the process that involves interactions and common
programmes among the 36 States of Nigeria. The Constitution of the
Federal Republic of Nigeria forbids members of one branch of government
to belong at the same time with another branch of government. For instance:
the *http://www.historylearningsite.co.uk/pres1.htm*President or the Cabinet
Ministers cannot be Senators or a member of the House of Representatives
or Supreme Court Judge while in office serving at a designated position in
any of the branches of government.

For government to attain full functionality there must be immense
cooperation in all the bodies and levels of government. However, contrary
to this stance, government may deteriorate and the branches of government
may loose ultimate legitimacy in the public arena. Thus, bargaining and
negotiation are commonplace for government survival.

The President cannot dissolve Congress. The President is expected to
present to Congress Bills as proposal that Congress maybe deem to favour
in legislations. Congress can either pass or return the proposal back to the
President for amendment. The President lacks both the power and the
constitutional means to compel Congress to respond favourably. Also, it
is required by law for the President to present the Federal government's
annual budget to Congress. The President does not require the support
of Congress to be effective; however, the President needs the support of
congress to maintain credibility with the public. The structure of Nigeria

Government has been so diffused, as against, concentrated; thus her structure of governance warrants common cooperation in all branches and levels of government.

In Nigeria Horizontal Federalism, each State is legally equal with other states in the federation regardless of location, size, and time of State origination. However, Bowman (2004), asserted that there are de facto asymmetry that exists among States whereby their relative influence within the federal structure varies. Thus, the Nigerian Constitution establishes State-to-State conduct in an effort to produce a functioning federal system, one in which State-to-State issues can be accommodated and Central Government can intervene, if necessary, to minimize conflict.

It is noteworthy, to indicate that the States do not need the approval of the Central Government to establish connections with other States. States are fully eligible to have the freedom to create interstate linkages. States compete with each other when they seek the same scarce objective. Thus, this initiative has contributed to the formulation of optimum efficiency in the federal system as a whole. Since the Framers will agree that the constitution is not perfect as drafted, the extent of State autonomy has been from time to time a subject of debate. Thus, some critics will argue that the Nigerian Government practice unitary system of government because of the way they perceived the balance of power has tilted firmly in the direction of the Central Government. However, it can be counter argued by another school of thought that the growth of the central power has not been monotonic, regardless of power imbalance; and thus, States remain constitutionally legitimated and imbued with their sovereignty.

As observed in Nigerian interstate cooperation, competition which is looked at as an antithesis of rivalry was seen as a plausible State-to-State behavior in the federal system. States also share common problems and build alliances and networks with each other. Thus, the cooperative behaviors between States that has been observed in the Nigerian context can be surmised as States working together toward a common joint pursuit for a particular objective and goal. As a result, when States act as allies rather than rivals, multistate administrative structures are usually created.

Thus, this opens avenues for interstate relationships that require trained and qualified administrators to work across State boundaries. McQuire & Agranoff (2003) asserted that this type of horizontal connections increase the opportunities for cross-jurisdictional collaborative management.

Vertical Federalism:

The Constitution guarantees the separation and existences of powers between States and Central Government. However, the States cannot be independent from the Central Government as they simply would not survive. The uniqueness of the system is the ability of the States to be interdependent and at the same time, be interactive with the Central Government in complex financial and administrative patterns. The Central Government is required to provide a participatory Democratic Government, preserve the territorial integrity of the States, and provide protection and assistance in times of domestic upheaval. The State Governments, on the other hand, consider proposed constitutional amendments and provide the machinery for conducting elections for president and members of Congress.

In Nigeria, each of the 36 States has its own position of legal autonomy and political significance. The constitution set up a division of power between the Federal and State Governments which initially limited the federal unit to the fields of defense, foreign affairs, the control of the currency and commerce between the States. This division of power has been eroded over the years so that today the Federal Government has functions that have been greatly extended and touch on the lives of all aspects of Nigerian citizens in all States of the federation.

Regardless of this expansion of federal power, the States continue to be very important political centers in government activity. However, States could take greater responsibility that could affect reduction in federal authority. The importance of the Nigerian States as legal entities is considerably enshrined in the Constitution. Today, most of the civil and criminal laws that govern Nigerian lives are State laws. State laws also cover family law, Sharia law, some traffic and commercial laws. The States have important regulatory functions, laying down many of the rules that businesses must observe. States have extensive powers of taxation and combined with Local Governments within each State spend huge sums of money on social welfare, education, health and hospitals. States have considerable constitutional and legal autonomy on how they fulfill their role as indicated in Chapter 11Fundamental Objectives and Directives Principles of State Policy of the Constitution:

> "The Constitution of the Federal Republic of Nigeria indicated that "whereas, the State shall foster a feeling of belonging and of involvement among the various people of the Federation, to the end that loyalty to the nation shall override sectional loyalties. The State shall abolish all corrupt practices and abuse of power. The State shall, within the context of the ideals and objectives for which provisions are made in this Constitution. harness the resources of the nation and promote national prosperity and an efficient, a dynamic and self-reliant economy; control the national economy in such manner as to secure the maximum welfare, freedom and happiness of every citizen on the basis of social justice and equality of status and opportunity; without prejudice to its right to operate or participate in areas of the economy, other than the major sectors of the economy, manage and operate the major sectors of the economy; without prejudice to the right of any person to participate in areas of the economy within the major sector of the economy, protect the right of every citizen to engage in any economic activities outside the major sectors of the state economy."

If State's laws append against the Constitution, the Supreme Court can declare them unconstitutional. If these laws conflict with valid federal laws then the Supreme Court can take the same course of action. If the Supreme Court decides that a law passed by Congress violates the rights of States, that law can also be declared unconstitutional. Federalism is still a potent force in Nigeria and it continues to draw its vigour from the desire at a political level to decentralize political power.

The structures of Central Government incorporate mechanisms to protect the rights of component States. The Nigerian legislative body is bicameral in nature, that is, the upper house (the Senate) is often used to represent the component States while the lower house (the representative) represents the people of the nation as a whole. In the federal upper house each State is represented by an equal number of senators irrespective of the size of its population. The members of an upper house are directly elected by the people of the State in the constituent they represent. The lower house of a federal legislature is also usually directly elected, with proportion to population in the State. In Nigeria, there are special procedures for amendment of the federal constitution. For instance, the federal structure guarantees that the self-governing status of the component States cannot be abolished without their consent. An amendment to the constitution of the Federal Republic of Nigeria and can only be ratified by two-thirds of either the State legislatures before it can come into effect.

The major limitations on States power are their relative lack of financial resources compared with those of the Federal Government. The material resources of the nation are harnessed and distributed as best as possible to serve the common good. No State, can tax as effectively as the Federal. The Federal Government has used State and Local Government as agents to administer the collection of taxes mainly from the harnessed natural resources and as such has the ability to keep the States concerned in check. In theory this gives the Federal Government a great deal of power over the States. In reality, it is in the interests of all those involved to work positively together especially when the sums of money involved are so vast.

However, States which have suffered from a natural disaster and cannot begin to meet the monetary needs required to cope with that disaster can be declared a "disaster area" by the Federal Government and receive financial support to cope with the problems presented. In most disasters, financially, the Local and State Governments could not cope with these disasters but the federal authority can. The current system helps to build a relationship between the States and the Central Government but it has lead to a powerful move towards Centralized Government.

Federalism is a dynamic instrument that is constitutionally formulated to projects the objectives of societal values to governance and it is required to be flexible enough to adapt to the circumstantial constitutional changes.

Federalism as a system of government has a clear decentralization of power to the States as enacted in the constitution.

The fundamental principles that warranted the practice of federalism in Nigeria are:

- Federations may foster peace and prevent wars among States.
- Federations can promote economic prosperity among States
- The constitutionality of federalism protects individual sovereignty no matter their State of origin.
- Federations can facilitate States objectives and programs.
- The system of federalism assists in protecting the political order, jurisprudence, adequate legislatures, and citizen's right.

The Nigerian Preferences of Federalism as a System of Government:

- As a result of the historic diversity of Nigeria as a nation, Nigeria federalism approach can be classified as "work in progress" and from the period of the end of the Nigerian Civil War and the several military juntas coupe-de-tats and the return of civil and democratic federalism system of governance, Nigeria has since pre-empted a continued work in progress in building a formidable and strong system of federalism. Nigeria has engaged herself through the dedicated works of the leaderships with enormous socio-economic specialization and tolerance, her well-structured private and public educational institutions, political structures, economic developments on several levels, traditional and religious structures. Thus, federalism as a system of governance can be seen in a basis of strong unity that respond favorably to civil and human rights abuses, ethnic and religious fundamentalist disputes, and curtailment of secessionist movements.

- Federalism as a system had propagated opportunities for citizens' participation in political engagements with structures in place for adequate checks and balance and to formulate laws and amendments that harnesses the integrity and creativity of her citizens to build a viable nation for all. As a result, without a careful balance between the powers and duties allocated to the Central Government and the State Governments, there will be no federalism. However, critics of the Nigerian federalism maintain that this balance has been disrupted by the excessive powers allocated to the Central Government, at the expense of the States Government.

- The present proposal in the Constitution states that the Central Government controls the properties and natural resources rights of the States. Thus, I will argue that the Central Government has gone too far; rather than restoring balance of equity by allowing the States in control of their alienable rights of properties and natural resources that encourages friendly economic competition among States that will encourage growth and development. Thus, critiques argue that the Central Government will be more progressive if the States were levied based on an agreed percentage of their disposed domestic properties and natural resources. However, as acknowledged, the Central Government rather simply overbalance on their favors and left the States with administrative responsibilities.

- Nigerians are committed to the federal system as the best political arrangement that guarantee unity, peace, stability, and reliable governance that protects her multi ethnicity and religious groups in all their ramifications. Under the federalism, citizens are guaranteed a formidable international and foreign influence and protection from undue advantage by others. While, weaker and minority constituents without viable resources are assured with development, protection, and representation as endowed in the constitution.

- Under the Nigeria Federalism approach, elections are not based on a simple majority practice alone because it is intended to ensure that candidates with narrow agendas do not dominate the political platform. Thus, scoring a simple majority, to ensure reliability and acceptability, a presidential candidate, must score 25% of the votes cast in two-thirds of the 36 States of the Federation. This is equally applicable to State Governors, Senators, and Representatives.

- To move government closer to the people, Nigeria with 774 Local Governments Council Members were elected according to constitutional provisions and electoral laws to represent the people in their Local Government constituents. Their functions among others, is to ensure that resources get to the people in the communities they serve.

- According to the federal constitution, police and military are controlled by the Central Government leadership. The President of the Federal Republic of Nigeria must appoint a Minister into his cabinet from each State of the Federation even if no single vote was cast in his favour from that State. This ensures that no State is left out of decisions making process in the federal level.

- Nigeria's official language is English, a language of choice. However, the constitution guarantees the right to use any of the indigenous languages, as may be necessary, to transact business without discrimination.

Nigerian federalism model is sensible and adequately designed but not perfect. However, with the new democratic practice in place, the citizens were fully committed and participate in the political decision-making process of the nation. As a nation that is well diverse culturally and ethnically, attempts were made to prepare her population in political inclusiveness which is fundamental in building a formidable democracy that encourages and protects freedom of speech. The best form of federalism engages in different political interest groups that ensure local and broader national issues on healthcare, education, employment, and freedom to all. Historically, Nigeria is a land of peace and unity. However, despite her multi-ethnic divide she has managed to maintain respect in the world stage. Thus, encourages over the years, the principle of political change that foster a sense of social justice within the ethnic groups. It is the interest of Nigeria as the largest populated country in Africa to always seek lasting peace and prosperity through her fundamental practice of federalism that espouses the sharing of burdens of the nation social, political, and economic implications. The nation should not only seek a systematic changed for nation's prosperity and lasting peace, but also, institutional changes with moral responsibility for the future generations of the country.

The practice of federalism in the 21st century in Nigeria must not be marginalized but be inclusive and open in all levels of government. Mature respect and trust among political leaders and the citizens they purported to serve will enhance the cause of true and vibrant federalism that is needed to make a larger difference in the world stage. The aspiration of the formation of genuine federalism approach in governance in Nigeria is tantamount to a lasting political solution for a country that yarn for equity and justice for all her citizens.

Federalism can be notably remarkable in accordance with the written constitution of Nigeria, if political power sharing are implemented responsibly and resourcefully among regional and local constituents from the 36 States. Hence, Local and State Governments should be independently governed without any intervention by the Central Government because equity under the constitution must uphold the rule of laws in a true democracy. A drafted constitution of a nation, like Nigeria, serves as a prototype of a system of how the nation should be governed and demands the change of attitudes of the leaders to accomplish the will of the people as mandated. Federalism in Nigeria will only succeed when the citizens from all ethnicity and demography share the resources and the security of the nation in equitably and fairness. A leader with a political power without moral value is like a "paper tiger". A federalism approach demanded the protection of all citizens and be treated with fairness, decency, and dignity.

Federalism as a political system endowed the governance with powers that are mending to be divided between the Central Government and State and Local Governments. The drafted constitution formulated this power sharing arrangement between the State and the Local Governments and stated their functions as to act independently in certain areas of governance.

For example, State and Local Governments have exclusive powers to issue licenses, provide for public health, and conduct elections.

Advantages of Federalism:

1. all provinces has political, social, and economic problems peculiar to the region itself. Provincial government representatives live in proximity to the people and are most of the time from the same community, so that, they are in a better position to understand these problems and offer unique solutions for them. For example, traffic congestion in Badagry Express road in Lagos State is a problem that can be best solved by the Local Government authorities in the areas, that are experts in the demographics of the area than by someone in the Central Government in Abuja making all the decisions.

2. Federalism offers representation to different populations. Citizens of various States may have different aspirations, ethnicity and follow different cultures. The Central Government can sometimes overlook these differences in diversities and adopt policies which cater to the majority. Thus, it is the responsibility of the State Government to intervene to protect the rights of the minorities by formulating policies pertaining to the State or Local needs of the people. State Governments have the freedom to adopt policies which may not be followed nationally or by any other State.

3. Division of work between the Central and the State Governments leads to optimum utilization of resources. The Central Government can concentrate more on international affairs and defense of the country while the State Government can cater to the local needs.

4. In federalism there are flexibilities for innovation and experimentation. For example, some Local Governments can have different approaches to bring reforms in any area of public domain, be it in health or in education. The comparison of the results of these policies can give a clear idea of which policy is better and thus, can be adopted in the future.

Disadvantages of Federalism:

1. sharing of power between the Central and the States government include both advantages and disadvantages of federation. Sometimes, there are overlapping of functions and subsequent confusion regarding who is responsible for a specific function.

2. Federal system of government is very expensive as more people are elected to office in both at the State and the Central Governments. Thus, it is often said that only rich countries can afford it. Too many elected representatives with overlapping roles may also lead to corruption and sometimes confusion.

3. Federalism leads to unnecessary competition between different regions. There are rebellious State Governments against the Central Government. Both scenarios pose a threat to the countries' integrity.

4. Federalism promotes regional inequalities. Natural resources, industries, employment opportunities differ from State to State. Hence earnings and wealth are unevenly distributed. Rich natural resources States offer more opportunities and benefits to its citizens than poor States with so called insignificant natural resources. Thus, the gap between rich and poor States widens.

5. Federalism can make the State Governments selfish and concerned only about their own region's progress. For example, Abia State Government non-citizens employee eviction by default from State jobs. Also, it is widely believed that the Abia State Government policies were formulated to the detriment of other States Government constitutional rights. For example, pollution from a State which is promoting industrialization in a big way can affect another state which depends solely on agriculture and cause crop damage.

6. Federalism does not eliminate poverty. Even in Lagos, the most populated and influential State in Nigeria, there are poor neighborhoods. The reason for this may be that during policy framing, it is the intellectuals and not the masses who are invited

by the Local Government. These intellectuals may not understand
the local needs properly and thus, policies might not yield good
results.

Due to the importance of federalism as a system of governance, the
advantages and disadvantages of federalism will be elaborated further in
the subsequent chapter.

Synopsis of the History of Nigeria Origin and the Choice of Federalism

The beginning of British Colonisation of Nigeria was when the British Prime Minister, Palmerston appointed John Beecroft as Nigeria first British Consul in 1849. Among the responsibilities of John Beecroft was the enforcement of a one-sided agreement for the protection of the interests of British traders and signing of the protection treaties that led to direct colonialism. The protection treaty is stated as follows:

- "The British majesty hereby undertakes to extend to them (Protected Peoples) and the territory under their authority and jurisdiction her gracious favour and protection."
- "The protected people were prohibited from entering into any correspondence, agreement or treaty with any foreign power or nation except with the knowledge and sanction of Britain."
- "Britain had exclusive jurisdiction, civil and criminal over Britons and British protected subjects in the protected territory and the authority was exercised by the British Consul."
- "Any disputes between the 'native' chiefs themselves or between them and British Citizens or foreign traders had to be submitted to the British Consul."
- "Native Chiefs were bound to act on the advice of the British officers in matters relating to the administration of justice, the development of the resources of the country, the interests of commerce or in any matter in relation to peace, order and good government and the general progress of civilisation."

In 1885, the British established the protectorate of the oil river which later became the Niger Delta Protectorate. As various quarrels and disputes ensue between British traders and officials on the one hand and the people in the protectorate on the other hand, the British invaded, conquered, and colonised individually the following kingdoms in Nigeria.

In 1894, during the NaNa war, the Itsekiri and Benin Kingdoms were conquered. In 1894 to1914, the following kingdoms were conquered: Isoko and Urhobo Kingdoms; Efunrun, Orokpo, Etua, and Ozoro kingdoms; Ezeonum, Amai, Iyede, and Oleh kingdoms. In 1890 to 1905, most of the Igbos and the Ibibios kingdoms gave up their lands without and hardy fight with the British; while, between 1895 and 1905, Okrika, Aboh, Aro, Ezza kingdoms gave the British some resistance before they were conquered. In 1861 to 1914, Lagos, Ijebu, and Egba kingdoms were conquered by the British.

Most of the North was under the Sokoto Caliphate in the 19th Century, with the exception of Borno and Middle Belt. In 1885 to 1899, the British operated the Royal Niger Company. In 1899, the Royal Niger Company charter was abrogated and a protectorate of Northern Nigerian was proclaimed in 1900 by the British to forestall German and French occupation of the Northern Nigeria.

The British conquest began in Northern Nigeria in 1901 to 1903 in the following kingdoms: Bida, Adamawa, Bauchi and Gombe, Zaria, Kano, and Sokoto Caliphate. Between the periods of 1903 to 1906, the British consolidated the Northern Kingdoms into Northern Protectorate. In 1900 the Southern Protectorate and the Colony of Lagos were amalgamated under the title "The Colony and Protectorate of Southern Nigeria." However, since 1901, Lord Frederick Laggard who was the High Commissioner of the Protectorate of Northern Nigeria also amalgamated the two separate protectorates of South and North in 1914. During the period 1900 to 1906, the Governor of the Protectorate of Southern Nigeria, Lord Lugard, exercised full executive powers and was also the legislature. This applied to the Protectorate of Northern Nigeria from 1900 to 1914. The Governor in each case made laws by proclamation. Such proclamation was, however, subject to approval by the British Government. In 1914, a Legislative

Council was created for the protectorate and was constituted as officials of government.

The Colony and Protectorate of Southern Nigeria, and the Protectorate of Northern Nigeria, were amalgamated, and ruled by one Governor-General, Lord Lugard, in 1914. The Legislative Council of the Protectorate was restricted to making laws for the Protectorate alone, whilst the Governor-General made laws for the whole country.

After the amalgamation, the two protectorates were separately administered; thereby, created disparities in the socioeconomic and political levels of development. The British colonialists and the Nigerian Nationalist were desirous of a system of government that would neutralize the potential threats and trust among the protectorates. The British Colonialists and the Nationalists eventually found a mutual but tacit agreement of expression in the federal system of government. This foster the demand for statehood by the Nationalists; as a result, the newly found germane for an Independence State was faced with simultaneous conflicting demands for territorial integration. This situation was dealt with by political leaders of Nationalist Independence movements (NIM) and colonial administrators alike who found in the federal solution—a Federalism Approach.

The Nigerian adoption of the federal system was not as a strategy to manage problems of pre-independence period but more importantly as an enduring strategy that could help detonate a major source of threat and promote trusts to the future political consolidation and stability of an independent Nigeria.

In 1922, a constitution revoking the 1914 constitution was promulgated under Governor Hugh Clifford. The underpinning of the Constitution shows a Nigerian Legislative Council was constituted, but its jurisdiction was limited to the Southern Provinces, which is, the Colony of Lagos and the Protectorate of Southern Nigeria. The Governor was slated to be the legislative authority for the Northern half of the country. Also, an executive council was established for the whole country.

In 1939, Nigeria was divided into three separate regions: Northern, Western, and Eastern Regions. On January 1st, 1946, Governor Arthur

Richards promulgated a new Constitution for Nigeria. The following are the features of the 1946 Constitution:

- The new Council was composed of the Governor as President, 16 officials and 28 unofficial (the latter including the four elected persons). This meant that for the first time the non-officials were more members of the council than the officials.
- The majority of the non-officials were elected or nominated by the Regional Legislatures which the 1946 Constitution also brought into bare. This meant that the unofficial majority were not subject to the Governor's control.
- The Regional Houses were not competent to legislate, even for their own Regions. They could only consider bills affecting their regions, and make recommendations or pass resolutions for the central legislature in Lagos to consider. It was the latter only that could pass legalization.

The introduction of the elective principle by Huge Clifford Constitution of 1922, earmarked the first political party in Nigeria in 1923 which was the Nigeria National Democratic Party (NNDP) under the leadership of Herbert Macaulay who was popularly referred to as the father of Nigeria Nationalism. The three seats allocated to Lagos in the legislative council were won by the party (NNDP) in the election held in 1923. Since the Northern and the Southern parts of the country were ruled as separate entities in spite of the amalgamation of 1914. The North was not represented in the legislative council and the legislation for that part of the country was by imperial proclamation, a form of **indirect rule**.

Bernard Bourdillion, the Governor-General initiated and laid the foundation of federalism in Nigeria in1939 by creating three provinces and formulated the practice of the indirect rule in the North. He was later succeeded by Arthur Richards, who in 1946 introduced a new constitution that became the Richard's constitution of 1946 that ended the indirect rule and formulated the introduction of regionalism. It was in that same year that Northern and Southern sections of the country were effectively brought under the national government. Regionalism in 1946 did not translate to the emergence of federalism. Nigeria was considered a unitary state. However, in 1951, the unitary system was changed by Macpherson who formulated the Macpherson constitution that promulgated the fundamental relationship needed between the British Colonialists and the entire people of Nigeria.

The following rules in the Macpherson Constitution are as follows:

- The 1951 constitution came into being after an unprecedented process of consultation with the peoples of Nigeria as a whole. In accordance with the directives of the Legislative Council, meetings and consultations were held at (a) villages (b) districts (c) divisional HQs (d) and provinces (e) regions and (f) the national conference.
- The reports of each region from villages to other districts were then submitted to the Legislative Council. The reports and recommendations were reviewed by a drafting committee of the Legislative Council and published in October 1949.
- On 9 January, 1950, a General Conference of representatives from all parts of Nigeria started meeting in Ibadan to map out the future system of government in Nigeria with the recommendation of the Regional Conference as the working documents.
- The General Conference was composed of 25 unofficial members drawn from the earlier regional conferences as representatives of the three regions, 25 unofficial members from the Northern Legislative Council, 3 official members and the non-voting Chairman who was the Attorney-General of Nigeria. The Conference rose on 29 January, 1950 with recommendations which were accepted and implemented by the Governor of Nigeria.
- The new Constitution represented a major advance on the existing state of legislative competence of Nigerians by (i) introducing elected majorities in the Central Legislature and (ii) in the Regional Houses of Assembly (iii) endowing the Legislative Houses with

independent legislative power in many areas of state activity and (iv) establishing a Federal System for Nigeria for the first time.

- The elected majorities in each Regional House were as follows: North—elected 90, non elected—14, West—elected 80, non-elected—7, East—elected 80, non-elected 8.

- The modes of election were a combination between direct and indirect elections. The Central Legislature had 136 elected members and 13 nominated members. Of these, 68 were from the North and 34 each were respectively from the East and West. The representatives of the Regions in the Central Legislature were elected by the Regional Legislatures from amongst themselves.

- This marked the first formal introduction of Federalism into Nigeria. Thus, the Conference indicated that: "We have no doubt at all that the process already given constitutional sanction, and fully justified by experience, of devolution of authority from the Centre to the Regions should be carried much further so that a Federal System of Government can be developed." And that:

> "The Central Legislature and Executive must retain both residual and overall powers, but since the Central Legislature and Executive will themselves be made up of representatives of the Regional Legislatures and since the policy of greater regional autonomy is so widely accepted, we do not fear that there will be any desire at the Centre unnecessarily to interfere with purely regional legislation or administration".

The adoption of Lyttleton constitution of 1954 marked the beginning of the federalism in Nigeria. Since 1954, Nigerians accepted the article of faith by unofficial referendum that the federalism approach of governance is the best form of government for the country. It was confidently expected that the Regions felt that they had wide powers to run their own regional affairs and they are more likely and ready to co-operate with the other

Regions through their representatives in the Council of Ministers and the House of Representatives in serving the interest of Nigeria as a whole.

In 1954, direct elections, to elect, federal legislatures was first held in Nigeria. In 1958, all modes of indirect elections were abolished and withdrawn. While all elections in Nigeria, henceforth, were held by direct polls. In 1957, the Governors ceased to preside over the Executive Councils in the East and the West regions and in 1959 it extended to the Northern region.

In 1954, the office of Premier was created in the Regions; while, in 1957, the office of Prime Minister was established at the Central Government and the office of the Governor were enacted in the East and West respectively. In 1959, the office of the Governor was established in the North. Though, Subsequent changes were instituted to promulgate further the cause of a full independence preparation.

It should be noted that it was the coming together of these autonomous communities, empires, and kingdoms that gave rise to a Nigerian Federal Government and thereby formulated various States and the Constitution. In 1960, Nigeria had her first Independent Constitution and a revised Federal Republic Constitution in 1963 was enacted. This sacred document was carefully drafted by the Nationalists and the people representatives after series of negotiations and compromises in their various deliberations. The important features of the 1960 Constitution were the extensive powers granted the Regions, making them effectively autonomous entities. And, the inauguration of the first indigenous Governor General of Nigeria and subsequently, the first President of Nigeria, Dr. Nnamdi Azikiwe, who was considered an official representative of the Queen of England. However, the obvious differences between the 1960 and the1963 constitution was that in the 1963 constitution, the President of Nigeria was no more an official representative of the Queen of England; rather was fully head of the Federal Republic of Nigeria. Another phase of change, was the replacement of the Judicial Committee of the British Privy Council for the Supreme Court as the highest Appellate Court of Nigeria.

Some features in the 1960 and 1963 constitution indicating navel and true federal system composed of powerful and autonomous Regions and a Central Government with limited powers:

- Each Region has its own separate Constitution, in addition to the Federal Government Constitution.
- Each region had its own separate Coat of Arms and Motto, from the Federal Government.
- The Regional Governments had Residual Power; for example: where any matter was not allocated to the Regions or the Federal Government, it automatically became a matter for Regional jurisdiction. Thus, apart from items like Aviation, Borrowing of moneys outside Nigeria, Control of Capital issues, Copyright, Deportation, External Affairs, Extraction, Immigration, Maritime Shipping, Mines and Minerals, Military Affairs, and Para-Military, Posts and Telegraphs, Railways. Other important and significant areas that permit the Regions equal rights to legislate and operate are: Arms and Ammunition, Bankruptcy and Insolvency, Census, Commercial and Industrial Monopolies, Combines and Trusts, Higher Education, Industrial Development, the Regulation of Professions, Maintaining and Securing of Public Safety and Public Order, Registration of Business Names, and Statistics.
- Separate Regional Judiciaries and the power of the Regions to establish, not only High Courts, but also Regional Courts of Appeal.
- The Regions had their own separate electoral commissions for Local Government elections. However, the Chairman of the Federal Electoral Commission was the statutory Chairman of the State Commission.
- The Revenue Allocation system under the 1963 Constitution was strictly based on derivation.

The resource control was duly recognised and implemented in the 1960 and 1963 Independence and Republican Constitution. The Regional

Constitutions, in the 1960 and 1963 Constitutions, described each Region as a sole governing Region of the Federal Republic of Nigeria whereby adequate provision were made to guarantee the economic independence of the Regions, thus avoiding the hollowness of a self-governing status. As a result, consistently with a Federal character of a country like Nigeria, with diverse and stringent demography, the basis of revenue allocation was strictly derivative. Thus, according to Section 140 of the 1963 constitution which made provision for the sharing of the proceeds of minerals, including mineral oil, stated that:

> "There shall be paid by the Federal Government to a Region, a sum equal to fifty per cent of the proceeds of any royalty received by the Federation in respect of any minerals extracted in that Region and any mining rents derived by the Federal Government from within any Region."

For the purposes of this section, the continental shelf of a Region was deemed part of that Region which is totally consistent with international law. In fulfillment of the derivation provision, Section 136(1) of the 1963 constitution indicated that 30 per cent of general import duties were paid into a distributable pool for the benefit of the Regions. With regard to import duties on petrol, diesel oil and tobacco, the total sum of import duty collected less administrative expenses, were fully payable to the Region for which the petrol or diesel oil or tobacco was destined. A similar provision was made for excise duty on tobacco. With regard to produce provision such as: cocoa, palm oil, groundnuts, rubber and hides and skin, the proceeds of export duty were shared on the basis of the proportion of that commodity that was derived from a particular Region. Thus, the derivative of the allocation of revenue and the proportionate share of such proceeds went to the Region for operating bases.

It can be argued that the North was always a reluctant partner in the creation of an Independent Federal Republic of Nigeria. The Northern delegations were strictly on shared equal equity in revenue allocation. As aforementioned, at the National Conference at Ibadan, the Northern delegates declared adamantly that they would not be part of Nigeria, unless they were allocated at least 50 per cent of the seats in the Federal Legislature. In other words, they demanded and got not less than the combined number of seats of both the Eastern and Western Regions.

In 1947, the Nigerian first Prime Minister after independence from Great Britain, Sir Abubakar Tafawa Balewa, stated that "Nigeria had existed as one Country only on paper, and that it was still far from being considered as one country, much less think of it as united." While, another Freedom Nationalist and founder of Action Group and Premier of Western Region, Chief Obafemi Awolowo stated that: "Nigeria is not a nation. It is a mere geographical expression. There are no 'Nigerians' in the same sense as there are 'English', 'Welsh', or 'French'. The word 'Nigerian' is merely a distinctive appellation to distinguish those who live within the boundaries of Nigeria from those who do not. There are various nationals or ethnical groups in the country." These remarks can be opined as been made from observation of disunity, distrust, and acrimony within the Nationalists Movement that were seeking independence from British Colonialist.

Federalism, Nigerian Choice as enacted in the constitution

It has been noted that at the end of the First National Conference in 1950 held by the representatives of Nigerian Nationalists and Colonialists, the delegations opted unanimously for Federalism.

The two main criteria that are taken into consideration for had chosen federalism as a system for Nigeria:

- When a country is multi-lingual and also consisted of diverse communities that have developed divergent of ethnicities and cultures, the constitution must be federal to function equitably,
- When a country is multi-lingual, the constitution must be federal, and the constituent states or regions must be organised on the basis of linguistic similarities.

Sir Ahmadu Bello, founder of Nigeria People Congress (NPC) Premier of the North Region, stated the most eloquent cases for true federalism:

"Many years ago there was no country called Nigeria. What is now Nigeria consisted of a number of large and small communities and kingdoms all of which were different in their outlook and norms. The advent of the British and of Western education has not materially altered the situation and these many and varied communities have not knit themselves into a composite unit . . . . Whatever Nigerians may say, the British people have done them a great service by bringing all the different communities of Nigeria together."

However, Chief Obafemi Awolowo's aforementioned assertion has been proven accurate despite the Inter-ethnic intolerance which has become chronic over the years, confirms that we are a country of many mutually distrustful nations, as is evident from the clashes we have experienced since the return of civil democratic rule in 1999. Thus, it is clearly proven that Nigeria needs a federal system that incorporate a separate and autonomous existence as States, while unifying the States through a Federal Central Government exercising some basic powers and running some common services for the good of all.

Federalism is an arrangement whereby powers within governments of a country are shared between a Federal or Central Authority, in—conjunction with and a number of State Governments in such a way that each unit as a State, including this Central Authority, existed as a government separately and independently from the other. In a federation, each government enjoys autonomy, a separate existence and independence of the control of any other government. Thus, the Central Government and the State Governments are autonomous in their respective authorities with a form of vertical or horizontal relationships with each other as enacted in the constitution.

Chief Anthony Enahoro asserted in one of his speeches he gave to the 5th Yoruba Convention in Houston, USA, indicated that the founding fathers of Nigeria agreed on a Federation of Nigeria composed of geographical regions structured on assumed compatibility rather than false protestations of uniformity, which was based on recognition and validation of the essentiality of equity among our various nationalities that foster on the provisions for the future creation of new regions and the democratic process that validate the protection of minorities over the power swell of the majority. He indicated that despite the structured federal approach, the unintelligible mistake of our founding fathers was realistically the issue of embracing the English, a foreign language, as the national medium of communication in attaining to the socio-economic activities, industry and commerce of the nation. Chief Enahoro argued that such contrived insertion in accepting or adopting English Language for the purpose of unity among various groups, for a nation to succeed, can be presumed to be the set back to our creativity and inventiveness as a nation in sciences, arts, literature, and political-economic development?

Chief Enahoro posited that for Nigeria Federalism to succeed in the 21st century, Nigerian has to be more realistic to change our countenance which includes accepting a Nigerian language as a spoken unified language of choice for the nation. Thus, in the contrary, it means that Nigeria could face ultimate disintegration as a people. He also stated that upon strict application of the principle that in order to make a Nigerian omelets which is acceptable to alien palates, you must break our indigenous nation—eggs or resisting that in the long-run, you would have to seek your people's destiny outside Nigeria or that if Nigeria is to survive and fulfill our collective aspirations, we would have to work for a true federal system.

Chief Enahoro asserted that countries in Europe are going through identity and economic changes, but in Nigeria, we lack the alertness, understanding, and courage to expand on our boundaries of thought and overcome on our fears that define the structures that halt our complete unification for a true sense of federalism which is the basis for our Federalist chosen Government that lies in our history since the 19th century transformation that existed under the rule of law and democracy for far longer than most republics in the history of our race. Chief Enahoro indicated that his view for Nigeria is to return from her seemingly unitary practice to a consented inherent capacity for a true Federalism that accommodate multi-ethnic nationalities and their diversities without undermining national unity that embrace a common spoken Nigerian Language which was the focus of our founding fathers to adopt Federalism in the London Constitutional Conference of 1953.

Natufe, et al posited that Nigerians elected federalism as a system of governance for the following reasons:

Socio-Economic: To share cultural and economic values with Sovereign States in the union in providing a desirable larger access to domestic markets that will espouse a feasible secured access to land, air, and sea for the overall nation's development and growth and the further enhancement of the citizens' standard of living and welfare.

Political: To strengthen relations with fellow States in creating a mutual understanding and unity that will endure international respect and recognition.

Security: Nations decide to practice federalism in order to be able to protect itself from real or an imagined threat to its national security.

Natufe, et al asserted that the dynamism of Nigerian federalism manifested itself in the socio-economic policies of the States as they pursued and executed developmental strategies in congruity with their respective capabilities. Thus, the Northern province was able to manage its natural resources (hides & skins, and groundnuts) without any intrusion from the Central Government; the West did the same with its cocoa, and the East with their palm oil, etc. The various levels of government respected the basic tenets of federalism. According to Natufe, et al., States should managed administratively their economic affairs and were not dependent on the Federal Government

Federalism allows for the division of sovereignty between the Central Government and the States. We can overstate that the management of this dual sovereignty between the Central Government and the States makes federalism a complex political option since both are independent. Natufe, et al asserted that it is vital that the division of powers as stated in the constitution between the Federal Government and the States reflected the core uniqueness of the respective States without compromising the abilities of the Central Government to effectively govern the nation.

It is important that there should be conceived balance of powers maintained between the Central Government and the States in federalism, the contrary may be tantamount to the acrimonious imposition of power by the Central Government on the States which may be seen as a unitary system of governing. However, many observers may argue that the present practice of the Central Government in Nigeria has been nothing more than a unitary system because of their infringement on States' rights contrary to the constitution's enacted principle of federalism that was opted by the founding fathers of the nation in 1954.

This conscious decision that was promulgated by the founding fathers was designed to protect minorities over majorities in the population and to foster unity among the citizens of the States. Thus, Nigerians chose federalism as a system of government because of its fundamental tenets in principle and practice that was geared towards social equity and justice for all. Whereby, the survivability of Nigeria as a nation depends on the leadership of the Central Government, legislators, and the State Governments. These arms of government must have total respect and regard for the judiciary in the interpretation of the constitution and laws of the nation. To deviate from this premise, may be detrimental to the cause of freedom, unity, and trust that is needed for a true federalism to uphold in a democratic system like Nigeria.

The trajectory indicators that portray the prospects of changes in the central government and state governments' relations in the Federal Republic of Nigeria can be attributed to the forbearing of the States absorbing its role and powers to advise, alter, and administer programs that were formerly administered largely by the Central Government; and some programs administered by the States, were administered according to explicit, binding federal guidelines. For instance, the new Badagry expressway construction and the Metro rail-link corridor in Lagos has moved primary responsibility from the State due to broad guidelines from the Central Government that averted excessive costs in construction.

The other issue is the emerging sense from the Supreme Court of Nigeria and the Central Government that stayed aloof from the decisions upheld by some State Governments to enact the practice of Sharia Law in their States Constitution. Thus, inflated critics view that the Central Government was not willing to give broad opinion on matters that preempted the State Governments' action on issue that was regarded to be within the Constitutionality of the Federation.

One aspect of benefits from competition across governments in democratic institutions of a country is voters' amiableness to express their preferences and thereby influence their government. The closer the correspondence between a citizen's preferences and government policies the better the democratic functionality.

Direct Democracy:

This system of democracy has been practiced in Nigeria even before Nigeria as a country was formed. It is the oldest form of democratic government in the world. This direct democracy is regarded as the best form of government because it involved all citizens. Citizens meet to debate and decide on issues within their local commune. Such as: hamlets, clans, and villages before it reaches the kingdoms. Only the most unusual issues were brought before the Paramount Chiefs and Kings in the Kingdoms. This system of administration divided authority among manageable units. It allowed problems to be solved on the level where the problem originated. in other words, government closest to the people governed best. That was essentially federalism. Thus there is always a link between direct democracy and federalism. In the past, the various hamlets or clans meeting physically assemble together to form a direct democracy that is only feasible in a federalist system. Today, most people speak of direct democracy as citizens' initiatives and referenda instead of the towns, villages, and clans meetings that is so prevalent in the past.

Federalism as a Governmental structure in Nigeria had made governments more responsive to citizens' wishes and preferences thereby bringing them closer aligned to government policies. Although, this alignment can be viewed as imperfect but got the institutions on the right direction of democracy. Federalist Government determined both the sizes and composition of expenditures and constellation of taxes and fees that finances the Central and State Governments. This system comes with a price like any other. Perhaps, its largest cost is borne by the citizenry who have to participate in elections at several levels of government. However, the benefits from a greater alignment of citizen preferences and Government policies outweigh the costs.

Federalism can impose additional costs on communities where the migration of citizens from State to State creates negative externalities such as tax competition which erodes government revenue sources. Thus, there is no evidence, however, to suggest that these costs outweigh the benefits from citizens' migration. There is optimism to believe that there are benefits from mobility stemming from the increase in the degree of homogeneity of preferences and competition in creating an environment of efficiency in government. Thus far, federalism in Nigeria can be seen as an attractive option and proposition in seeking more responsiveness from the citizens and more efficient democratic institutions. It has been a challenging venture that our founding fathers had structured from the direct democracy. As a result, quitting is not an option; but to continue to design a formidable institutions that has the maximum potential in achieving a better tomorrow for the present and the future generations of proud Nigerians.

Most discussions of the Federalism begin with the Constitution. Thus, I will focus on three equally important provisions of the constitution. Firstly, The General Provision of Chapter 1, Part II, Section 10. The Government of the Federation or of a State shall not adopt any religion as State Religion." The purpose is to separate religious practices from State affairs. Our founding fathers may have envisaged that if religion is infiltrated into politics it would corrupt the system. The framers were assertive and outright in their foresights to claim the possibility to be free to disagree among each other as a fundamental choice of freedom. Ultimately, however, certain policy choices have to be made—even in a free society. In our society, we have sought to both limit the number of these decisions that must be made and to spread those choices out as widely as we can so that there is more room for experimentation and less opportunity for one faction to impose its will on another. This is why the framers viewed "the States" and "the people" as interchangeable. State policy will always better reflect the interests of its citizens than the Federal government can.

Secondly, The Fundamental Objectives and Directive Principles of State Policy, Chapter II, Section 14 (4) The composition of the Government of a State, a Local Government Council, or any of the agencies of such Government or Council, and the conduct of the affairs of the Government or Council or such agencies shall be carried out in such manner as to recognise the diversity of the people within its area of authority and the need to promote a sense of belonging and loyalty among all the people of the Federation. And, Section 15 (1, 2, 3): (1). The motto of the Federal Republic of Nigeria shall be Unity and Faith, Peace and Progress. (2). accordingly, national integration shall be actively encouraged, whilst discrimination on the grounds of place of origin, sex, religion, status, ethnic or linguistic association or ties shall be prohibited. (3). For the purpose of promoting national integration, it shall be the duty of the State to:

(a) Provide adequate facilities for and encourage free mobility of people, goods and services throughout the Federation.
(b) Secure full residence rights for every citizen in all parts of the Federation.
(c) Encourage inter-marriage among persons from different places of origin, or of different religious, ethnic or linguistic association or ties; and
(d) Promote or encourage the formation of associations that cut across ethnic, linguistic, religious and or other sectional barriers. Clearly the idea of divided sovereignty does not imply that states are free to do absolutely anything they want. They too are bound by the Constitution's constraints. But, as set forth the limitations on State power are designed to promote both the interstate mobility and the diversity of policy choices that undergird the Federalist model of ordered liberty.

And, section 17(1,2,3), (1). The State social order is founded on ideals of Freedom, Equality and Justice.

(2). in furtherance of the social order—

(a) Every citizen shall have equality of rights, obligations and opportunities before the law;
(b) The sanctity of the human person shall be recognised and human dignity shall be maintained and enhanced;
(c) Governmental actions shall be humane;
(d) Exploitation of human or natural resources in any form whatsoever for reasons, other than the good of the community, shall be prevented; and
(e) The independence, impartiality and integrity of courts of law, and easy accessibility thereto shall be secured and maintained.

(3). The State shall direct its policy towards ensuring that—

(a) All citizens, without discrimination on any group whatsoever, have the opportunity for securing adequate means of livelihood as well as adequate opportunity to secure suitable employment;
(b) Conditions of work are just and humane, and that there are adequate facilities for leisure and for social, religious and cultural life;
(c) The health, safety and welfare of all persons in employment are safeguarded and not endangered or abused;
(d) There are adequate medical and health facilities for all persons:
(e) There is equal pay for equal work without discrimination on account of sex, or on any other ground whatsoever;
(f) Children, young persons and the aged are protected against any exploitation whatsoever, and against moral and material neglect;
(g) Provision is made for public assistance in deserving cases or other conditions of need; and
(h) The evolution and promotion of family life is encouraged.

This provision requires that citizens of one State traveling or taking up residence in another State must be treated with all of the same legal protections as the citizens of the host State. In other words, the provision requires that all Nigerian citizens be treated as citizens of the State that they currently occupy. The purpose of inserting this provision in the constitution was to ensure that interstate mobility was possible for all Nigerians. This provision makes it unconstitutional for States to treat as null and void the actions of sister States. Thus, when a citizen of another State seeks employment or educational admission in another State, the citizen migrant will not in any circumstance of employment be terminated or refused employment or educational admission for any selfish political reasons due to the status of the migrant citizen not being an indigene or resident of the State. When residents married in one State seek a divorce in another state, the courts of that State may generally not refuse to dissolve the marriage on the sole ground that the marriage was solemnities under the laws of another state. In other words, the various states, in ratifying the constitution, agreed to disagree on some policy matters, but agreed to work together and not undermine the varying policy determinations of another state. This is both a check on and a protector of State power.

The provision is so important that it provides the theoretical basis for policy experimentation among the institutions of governance with regards to derivation. Although, our founding fathers recognized that the individual's rights were less threatened by the States than by the Federal Government and that, individuals had more opportunity to influence their State Government than the Federal Government to recognized that sometimes the best option for the individual who cannot abide by the government policies may move on to somewhere more tolerable to his sensibilities. Indeed this ethic was firmly entrenched in the Nigeria ideal from the early colonial period, where religious crusaders of various sects left their homeland to spread their various religious affiliations and exchange their goods and services in Nigeria.

The Islamic religion found home in the North; while Christianity religion, that is, the Catholics, the Anglicans, the Baptists, Protestants, and the Presbyterians were predominantly found in the East, West, and Middle Belt states. There were differences and social preferences among the religious groups in the 19th century; however, the framers and the religious leaders entered an agreement to respect those differences in the name of liberty and dignity for all.

Thirdly, Public Revenue, Chapter VI, Section 162 (2) The President, upon the receipt of advice from the Revenue Mobilisation Allocation and Fiscal Commission, shall table before the National Assembly proposals for revenue allocation from the Federation Account, and in determining the formula, the National Assembly shall take into account, the allocation principles especially those of population, equality of States, internal revenue generation, land mass, terrain as well as population density provided that the principle of derivation shall be constantly reflected in any approved formula as being not less than thirteen per cent of the revenue accruing to the Federation Account directly from any natural resources.

The Public Revenue was enacted to empower congress and the President of the Central Government to ensure that States revenue allocations were allocated in accordance with the constitution. States were emphatically authorized to claim their rights in formulating economic developments in Local Government areas with the provisions in the principle of derivation. The original understanding of this power distribution with regards to revenue allocation was simply to ensure that peace and mobility was maintained between the states and the central government in ensuring a free and equitable society.

Advantages and Disadvantages of Federalism as a System of Government in Nigeria

Advantages:

There is no one federal systems that are alike. Some systems are designed to have very different governmental structure than other federal systems based on the demography of the population of the country. The constitution is the mainframe in designing a federalism system by indicating the distribution of particular powers, and how the functionalities of the various governments' authorities are crucial in determining the way government works on different levels. A choice for federalism does not resolve or even address questions of how powerful different levels of government should function among each other.

A constitution can delineate the spheres of authority of each level of government; but there are precise unconsidered issues that are bound to arise. How the government deals with issues, and how the National Constitution allows for change that is important to peace, stability, and dynamism in a federal system. The choice of a federal structure does not itself dictate the resolution of the issues of change, but provide in the National Constitution a provision of the enforcement of laws and order that befit a federal system of approach in Nigeria.

Federalism offers a means of introducing essential features of the markets into politics. Federalism serves the dual purposes of allowing the range or scope for a national government activity. The efficacy of competitive federalism depends directly on the free movement of citizens from State to State that provide operative strength of migrant option in the system. Thus, the ability of citizens to migrate freely and shift investment and trade options across State boundaries, serves to limit political exploitation in the framework of the system.

In Federalism there is co-existence between the different levels of government and at the same-time function differently in regards to their various State Constitutions which exerts political spillover effects on the national scene. Federalized sovereign structure reduced the extent to which tribal identities in politics are transcended. Thus, under federalism, the Central Government is strong, but must not be allowed to extend beyond its constitutional limits.

In a federal approach, State Governments have political, social, and economic problems peculiar to the region they govern. State Government representatives live in the same community and in close proximity to the people they deem to serve. Thus, they are in a better position to understand the problems of the peoples they represent and offer unique solutions for them. For example, traffic congestion in Lagos Island and most of its' environs are some problems that can be best solved by the State Government, keeping local factors in mind, rather than by somebody living in Abuja. Federalism offers representation to different populations. Citizens of various States may have different aspirations, ethnicity and follow different cultures. The State Government authorities not only formulate policies that cater for the needs of the people; they also take into consideration local needs, tastes, and opinions of the citizens given due consideration by their state of mind.

In federalism, State Governments have the freedom to adopt policies which may not be followed nationally or by any other State. Divisions of responsibilities are portioned between the Central and the State Governments which in most case lead to optimum utilization of resources. The Central Government concentrates more on international affairs and defense of the country while the State Governments cater to the local needs of the people. Nigerians feel close ties to their home States as a result of personal cultural attachments and federalism maintains that connection by giving power to the States.

Federalism has room for innovation and experimentation; where State Governments can experiment policies with other States and the Central Government can learn from their successes and failures. For instance, two Local Governments can have two different approaches to bring reforms in any area of public domain. Thus, the fair collaboration of ideology, usually lead to comparison of the results of each policy that gave clear ideas of which policy is better to adopt in future. Being pragmatic, governing a diverse population in a country the size of Nigeria, is much easier to do because power is disseminated to Local Authorities. Thus, State and Local Authorities choose polices in collaboration to solve the people problems.

Federalism in Nigeria has led to political stability in removing Central Government from some contentious issue, the federal approach has allowed the Nigerian Government either civilian or past military Government to achieve and maintain stability because of their respect for the constitution. Federal systems encourages pluralism by expanding the levels of government (Central, States, and Local levels) and gave people more access and opportunities to get involved in their government. This system ensures the separation of powers between the levels of government and prevents tyranny. The constitution as adopted by the founding fathers, if one person or group took control of all three branches of the Central Government, federalism ensures that State Governments would still function independently. Federalism, therefore, fulfills the framers' vision of a governmental structure that ensures liberty for all Nigerians.

The federal system of a Central Government approach has resulted in a disparity, in equality, and participation. Criteria for schools, land-use, welfare, legal sanctions, and State expense are quite different among the States and Counties. The federal system allows for collaboration and friendly competition to take place among her citizen with the focus to value individual liberties and rights as citizens.

The Central Government upholds these rights and ensures nothing infringes upon them. As a result, the advantage of a strong and Centralized Government is the oversight and policing of its policies, such as: no Local

Government can set policies that violate these constitutional promises. Federalism ensures a balance of power whereby States can set laws and policies that the Federal Government checks. In addition, States send representatives to federal legislative bodies, such as Congress and the House of Representatives, to veto certain laws that do not seem beneficial to the States Constituency. Thus, both the Federal Government and States have a system of checks and balances, in which both must act in accordance with what is best for the country. Another benefit of federalism in Nigeria is a strong federal government that ensures a national military and para-military that will provide security to the boundaries of her nation and safety to all her citizens.

Federal laws of Nigeria were written and are enforced within the respective States in the federation. Federalism allows same currency system (Naira and Kobo) to be easy to manage and exchange in any part of the federation of Nigeria. Also, there is uniform immigration policies that are written and enforced by the central agency for the convenience of States. Trade Agreements formulated by the Central Government in a federalized system, gain international respect unlike trade agreements that are performed by a individual State. In a federal system each State can retain its own culture, style and language.

A State can have its own particular laws to suit its customs and religion. Each State is free to develop a policy position specific to the issues in its own area and the needs of its local constituents. The State Government is better placed than the Central Government to understand the mood of distant local communities in their States. In a federalized system the Central Government is free to focus on critical issues that may interfere with the stability, foreign policy, and economic progression of the federation, to enable the State Government have the capacity to deal more efficiently with the mundane issues of their constituents in the State.

Disadvantages:

It is often said that only rich countries can afford the practice of federalism. And, that too many elected representatives with overlapping roles from the State representatives may also lead to corruption. Federalism leads to unnecessary competition between different States which may create acrimony between States.

Federalism promotes States inequalities in distribution and allocation of natural resources, industries, employment opportunities. As a result of increases in unemployment from State to States, earnings and wealth are unevenly distributed. Rich States offer more opportunities and benefits to her citizens than poor States. Thus, widen wealth or poverty gaps between States. Federalism can encourage the State Governments to be selfish and only concerned the State with the welfare of her citizens alone. State Governments can formulate policies which might be discriminately to other States. Some critics may argue that federalism does not eliminate poverty and that the rights of minorities in some States are not being adequately protected.

In Federalism States lose their sovereignty to some degree to the Central Government; while local authorities are being manipulated by the State Government to achieve their political aspirations instead of the people needs. The federalist system can always lead to policy differentiation between States. Thus, without clear Central Government laws and policies, it can be confusing keeping up with what is allowed from State to State. Also, there are overlapping in jurisdiction between States and Central Government; as a result, there are confusion in some cases of which government is responsible for certain issue.

In the federal system the broad economic affairs is handled by the Central Government. However, considering the economic differences between each State of the federation, the Federal Government concern in dealing with the State economic affairs is holistic. The actions of the Federal Government may sometimes have differing effects in different States in terms of their economic development moving forward. As a result, citizens in some States are left more vulnerable with less support than citizens in other States. This can cause inequality, as opportunities and resources differ greatly from States. It can be difficult for patriotism and nationalism to develop since the individual culture, religion, and customs of each State is preserved and sometimes manipulated for selfish reasons by power driven politicians. Citizens of most States have differing opinions about how the federal government is consumed with broad policies that tend to pull the States often on different directions.

In Nigeria, federalism is still considered by many Nigerians as an approach of choice; but skeptical of her constitutional mandates. Most Nigerians were of the opinion that federalism is an effective tool of government that is designed by the framers to achieve peace and stability with a sustainable prosperous democracy

Critics on federalism argued that Nigeria practice of federalism is a myth because the governing approach is not within the constitutional mandate of federalism. They also asserted that even the constitution cannot dictate or set primary limits on where States or Federal Law will operate. Critics indicated that federalism does not protect minority rights in most States and the distributions of derivatives to States are inequitable at best. As a result, they further argued that these bedrock issues are disturbing to majority of the citizens. However, other school of thought posited the practice of federalism in Nigeria as been a viable and workable system of approach that fosters the separation of powers between levels of government. They argued that the system is not designed to right all wrongs of the nation; but, rather a work-in-progress that is a substantive manifesto designed to find an equitable solutions to the nation's problem.

As aforementioned, the federalism approach is very expensive. More representatives are elected to office in States and Central Governments with less accountability due to the overlapping functions in governments that sometimes makes it possible for representatives of various levels of government to gallivant and potion blames for failed policies among themselves. The populace are not too conversant with the function of federalism as an approach of governance, as a result, it can be stated that the populace are ignorant of the process that govern them. Citizens often ignore the presence and the lack thereof of the functionalities of their representatives, even-though, these governments representatives have lots of power to affect their lives and communities they tend to serve.

The Philosophy of Federalised Democracy In Nigeria

The practice of federalism in Nigeria can be claimed to be in existence since the functionality of the various kingdoms. Such instance is the Eko kingdom, the present day Lagos Mainland, was under the kingship of King Ado (1630-1669) first King of Lagos. Taxes were passed on to the Oba of Bini from the King in Eko until the British came and explained that there was no need to send taxes to Bini anymore especially as the Oba of Bini pay taxes to Britain. However, during the reign of King Akintoye (1841-1845 &1851-1853), the direct influence of the Oba of Bini on Eko (present day Lagos Mainland) ended when King Akitoye ceded Lagos to the British. There was direct democracy with a structured government before the arrival of the British and other European transients in Nigeria. Policies were originated from the bottom-up by the established kingdoms.

The chiefs and head of clans deliberated on issues that maybe considered policy shifts which may affect the people and the various communities at—large. Thus, rules and laws were enacted and sent to the king-makers (elder chiefs) for review and ultimately to the king's for rectification and approval. This basic idea behind our fore-fathers vision on direct democracy had translated to a new approach of governance "federalism". It can be reckon that the tenet of traditional law and rules were the order of resolving and negotiating conflicts and disagreements through peaceful methods rather than coercion or war.

During the British rule in Nigeria, some educated Nigerians intermingled with organizations like the Pan African Movement activists who are campaigning for change and the abolition from exploitation of the oppressed people of Africa. These scholars formulated a Nationalist Movement and requested for an independent self-rule of Nigeria.

However, the Nationalists Movement started formulating political parties of their own ovation. Some of the major defunct political parties were the National Council of Nigeria and the Cameroons (NCNC), the Northern People's Congress (NPC), and the Action Group (AG). in1951, self-government was constituted in the three regions, each of the regions was adversarial competitors and their dominant ideologies were based on ethnical and cultural divide. Hence, there were the plethora of complaints of exclusion and oppression by minorities in all the regions.

The founding fathers who are members of the Nigerian Nationalist Movement did not relent on the acrimony that was happening in the regions. They were bent on finding solutions to governance that will bring stability in the regions. The British Colonialist collaborated with the leaders of the movement to formulate a system that will be beneficial to the people of Nigeria. Thus, federalism was chosen based on the drafted Nigerian Constitution that was based on the federal system that recognises diversity in culture, language, and political allegiances. The factor of direct democracy resonated in this equation again as a measure of bringing the citizens closer to their leaders. In federal system as a structure of governance, power is disseminated and shared among level of government to attain an equitable socioeconomic phenomenon. These principles are the pillars on which the modern multi-ethnic and culturally diverse Nation and States were later created and governed. This principle of federalism approach was determined to protect pluralism and the rights of individual against over-powerful government.

The State of affairs in Nigeria after independence was highly envious and this was attributed to the potential contributions of the founding fathers ideology in drafting and enacting a formidable binding constitution with a daunting democracy and profound levels of governing institutions. Some of the notable Nigerians that formulated the Nigeria Constitution that finally, brought Nigeria independence from Britain were: Dr. Nnamdi Azikwe, Sir Tafawa Belawa, Sir Ahmadu Bello, Chief Obafemi Awolowo, Chief Anthony Enahoro, to mention a few. These "Greats" were equally essential and fundamental to the dreams that brought social change to the dependent Nigeria from the yoke of British greed, tyranny, injustice, invasion, and oppression.

The founding fathers total struggle for freedom propagated the principles of non-violence, non-interference, and respect for sovereignty. The forthrightness of the founding fathers can be learned by the present leaders of Nigeria; if only, they can eradicate selfishness and set good leadership qualities that are worthy of emulation by future generations of Nigerians. The political philosophies of the founding fathers embedded in the framework of the principles of federalism, if practiced, as enacted with the cradle of ethnic harmony and social equity for all Nigerians would make Nigeria, once again the proud envy of the world.

Recent federalist philosophers in Nigeria had argued on the issues of whether Nigeria has shifted from the founding father intent of federalism to unitary system; if Nigeria can sustain stability as the product of growth and development; the legitimate division of power between States and the Central Government; and the politics of distributive justice.

Based on the traditional values that are embedded in Nigerian cultures in pursing liberty, freedom, and opportunities for all citizens, the founding fathers did not require constitution retrenchment of different philosophy that favor a federal order for an independent sovereign state of Nigeria. Their constant patriotism and national character that makes us one nation and one people despite our ethnic and religion differences are lessons to learn from them.

Some of the reasons the founding fathers adopted federalism rather than secessionism are:

1. Federation may foster peace and justice through power sharing and at the same time, have a formidable union that can dissuade external aggression or a preemptive war.
2. Federation will promote economic development in the States by eradicating barriers to trade within the country and espousing adequate trade agreements that befits international trade protocol.

3. Federation will protect minority rights and entrust political authorities to facilitate measures of securities and ensure states sovereignty in accordance with the constitution.

4. Federation as a political system that is designed to formulates stability and social consciousness among States and the citizens within the States and securing common bonds and trust among all people within the federation.

5. Federation does not only protect citizens with shared values, it also, promotes the free-will of citizens' mobility from one State to another without any hindrances to transact or conduct their personal business.

Democratic Theory of Federalism in Nigeria:

As acknowledged in the previous chapters, federal political system accommodates the protection of minorities in the following ways: division of power and freedom of expression.

Division of Power:

The separations of government powers are assigned with different levels and responsibilities: The executive branch, legislative branch, and the judicial branch. The executive branches in the Central and State Governments are responsible for the administration of policies and enforcement of laws being enacted by the legislative and signed into law by the executive. The legislative branches are responsible for deliberating and making policies that will be formulated into laws. The judicial branches interpret the laws that the legislatures formulated. This democratic system of governance that is practiced in Nigeria is regarded as a horizontal approach. However, in a federalism system, there is another approach called the vertical system; whereby, separations of powers in government are shared between the Central, State, and Local governments.

In Nigeria, the division of powers in government were developed many centuries ago; even before the British invasion and colonization of Nigeria.

The various kingdoms were structured in a democratic format. The king was the executor and the head of the kingdom. The king-makers were the legislators that formulate laws that the King later certified. The chiefs and clan heads are responsible to the various fringes of governance within their clans and hamlets. Their structure of governing is both horizontal and vertical that fits the federalism approach of the modern era.

The modern era of the division of power has the infusion of the British constitutional doctrine due to the colonial administrator's influence in drafting the constitution with the Nigerian Nationalist Movement. The notable contribution of the British Constitutional doctrine in the 1960 Nigerian Constitution, among others, was the checks and balances that were factored into the division of powers approach in the constitution. This formidable piece assured that government powers at any level have to be controlled by an overlapping autonomous authority within the government. Thus, given the citizens the perpetual right to oversee government mismanagement and vote the incompetent leaders out of office.

As enacted in the 1960 Constitution of the Federal Republic of Nigeria, the Central and State Governments are separate but equal with different allocation of powers. The Central Government has the responsibilities of delegating powers, regulating immigration, grant diplomatic recognitions to other nations and protect the sovereignty of the nation. The Central Government cannot infringe on the rights of her citizens either by intruding into the citizens freedom of speech, freedom of the press, and freedom to assemble.

The Central Government cannot tax the State Governments. Hitherto, the State Governments have the power to protect and promote public health, public morals and decency. The State Governments cannot make treaties, print money, and deny the rights of citizens movement except ordered by the court. As a result of the Central and State Governments concurrent powers, both government can collect taxes, define crimes, condemn or take private properties for public use and enforce public safety and general welfare of the citizens with their various constituents. The governments cannot violate the rights of their citizens. In case there is an overlapping of laws between the State and Central jurisdiction, the Central law always takes precedence over the State Law.

This division of power is promulgated in a pronounced manner that no entity or person function in one authority or hold a position of functionality that is both vertical and horizontal. Thus, this theoretical framework of division of power in Nigeria system of government has infused respect for the citizens' rights, liberty, and justice and peace and tranquility for the nation.

Freedom of Expression:

Freedom of expression is protected by Article 39, Chapter IV of the Fundamental Right, of the Constitution of Nigeria, wherein the article qualifies this right, providing that "(1). Every person shall be entitled to freedom of expression, including freedom to hold opinions and to receive and impart ideas and information without interference. (2). Without prejudice to the generality of subsection (a) of this section, every person shall be entitled to own, establish and operate any medium for the dissemination of information, ideas and opinions: Provided that no person, other than the Government of the Federation or of a State or any other person or body authorised by the President on the fulfillment of conditions laid down by an Act of the National Assembly, shall own, establish or operate a television or wireless broadcasting station for, any purpose whatsoever. (3). Nothing in this section shall invalidate any law that is reasonably justifiable in a democratic society—

(a) For the purpose of preventing the disclosure. of information received in confidence, maintaining the authority and independence of courts or regulating telephony, wireless broadcasting, television or the exhibition of cinematograph films; or

(b) Imposing restrictions upon persons holding office under the Government of the Federation or of a State, members of the armed forces of the Federation or members of the Nigeria Police Force or other Government security services or agencies established by law.

Freedom of expression is a cornerstone of democratic rights and freedoms. In its very first session in 1946, before any human rights declarations or treaties had been adopted, the UN General Assembly adopted resolution 59(I) stating "Freedom of information is a fundamental human right and . . . the touchstone of all the freedoms to which the United Nations is consecrated." Thus, in Nigeria, freedom of expression is fundamental in enabling democracy to work. Public participation in political activities has promulgated citizens to exercise their right to vote effectively and participate in public forum decision-making. Freedom of expression practiced in Nigeria enabled citizens' dignity and enforced accountability in the democratic system. However, the new emerging internet opportunities and satellite broadcasting in Nigeria had envisaged new threats in individual freedom of expression. For instance, some of the dialogue on the Internet surely tests the limits of conventional discourse; such as, expression on the Internet can be unfiltered, unpolished, emotionally charged, sexually explicit, vulgar, and pornographic.

Thus, under Article 19 of the Universal Declaration of Human Rights and the recognition therein by the International Human Rights Law, goes on to say that the exercise of these rights carries "special duties and responsibilities" and may "therefore be subject to certain restrictions" when necessary "[if] or respect of the rights or reputation of others" or "[if] or the protection of national security or of public order (order public), or of public health or morals." Hitherto, freedom of expression in Nigeria is considered a viable right for all citizens to speak freely without any censorship. This term freedom of expression may be expressed as the act of seeking, receiving, and exchanging of information or ideas. However, this act can be subject to limitation when it interferes with the laws of the land, in such circumstances as being libelous, obscene, incitement, slander, and used for the purpose to committing crime. Nigeria was among the countries that ratified the Human Right international treaty and agreed to meet her obligations by implementing these provisions fully at the national level.

As acknowledged, freedom of expression is the right to freely say what one pleases, as well as the exchange of ideas and thoughts in any synchronised manner. Freedom of expression can also encompass the freedom to create and distribute movies, pictures, songs, dances, and all other forms of expressive communication. Freedom of expression is crucial in any democracy, because open discussions of political aspirants or candidates' vying for political offices are necessary for voters to make informed elections decisions. Citizens can influence social and economic changes on government policies through free discuss and expressions. Also, public officials are held accountable through criticisms that can pave the way for change. Alternatively, it can be argued that some limitation to free speech may be deemed compatible with democracy or necessary to protect it.

This classic example of refusing Biafra to secede from Nigeria may be argued as protecting freedom of speech and fundamental rights of all her citizens through truth, Justice, and unity. The Central Government protected freedom of speech because of the essential value in dialoguing and deliberating as a necessary virtue to process the search for truth and justice. The notion of freedom of expression is ultimately linked to the concept of democracy whereby the elected and appointed officials were mandated by the constitution to disclose public information to their electorates and avoid stifling criticism.

The Essential Theories in Nigerian Federalism:

The policy of federalism is the act of delegating responsibilities and decision making from the hierarchical or vertical structure in a system. The Federated Nigerian Constitution reflected personal authority to her citizens and the governing body. Indeed, it also, focused on the aspects of human behavior and moral as the guided efficiency for a system to succeed in a federalized government. The guided efficiencies are: *Planning*—thinking before acting; *Organising*—setting up policies and procedures for the behaviors of citizens and others; *Staffing*—recruiting innovational and inventive work force; *Controlling*—motivating all citizens to pursue their God giving goals and potentials. There are some theories that have some similarity with the federalised constitutional system in Nigeria that are worthy of discussion: **decentralised organisational theory, decentralised political theory, and fiscal and decentralised theory.**

Decentralised Organisational Theory:

Organisation theory is examined here primarily from a historical perspective that briefly summarises its evolution. The open-systems theory which is the dominant school of thought throughout most of the 20th century, is examined in greatest detail; while, organisational characteristics and structures are also reviewed.

1. Evolution

Modem organisation theory was rooted in the concepts of Max Weber and Henri Fayol. It was developed during the Industrial Revolution in the late 19th and early 20th centuries. Weber and Fayol believed that bureaucracies, staffed by bureaucrats, represented the ideal organizational form. They posited their argument on model bureaucracy based on legal and absolute authority, logic, and order. Weber and Fayol asserted that responsibilities for citizens and their leaders are clearly defined and behavior is tightly controlled by rules, policies, and procedures. In effect, Weber and Fayol's bureaucracy was designed to function like a machine; similar to the Nigerian constitution.

Weber and Fayol asserted that bureaucracy was arranged into specific functions, or parts, each of which worked in concert with the other parts to form a systematic or synchronised process. Weber and Fayol's theories of organisations, like other theorists of the period, reflected an indifferent and impersonal attitude toward the people in the organisation. Indeed, personal aspects of human behavior were considered unreliable and were viewed as a potential detriment to the efficiency of any system. However, the major issue that differentiates Weber and Fayol's views on bureaucracy that provided important insight into process efficiency, division of labor, and hierarchy of authority from the Nigerian constitutional bureaucratic system was the contributing and the reliability factors of human behavior in innovation and invention potentials of the system.

The adoption of the human centered approach as against the total mechanized approach of Weber and Fayol by the framers in the Nigerian constitution is another proof of the founding fathers thoughtfulness and devotion to diversity that embraced unity and justice for all Nigerians. The theoretical views of the framers were more supported by modern organisational theorists like the Hawthorne experiments that shed light on the function of human fulfillment in organisations. Primarily under the direction of Harvard University researcher Elton Mayo, the **Hawthorne Experiments** were conducted in the mid 1920s and 1930s. The results of the studies demonstrated that innate forces of human behavior may have a greater influence on organisational systems than do mechanistic incentive systems. The legacy of the Hawthorne studies and other organisational research efforts of that period was an emphasis on the importance of individual and group interaction, humanistic management skills, and social relationships that is prominent in the Nigerian federalist horizontal and vertical system.

The focus on human influences in the Nigerian System was reflected and mostly noticeable in the integration of Abraham Maslow's "hierarchy of human needs." This Maslow's theory had two important implications for the Nigeria organisation theory that the framers adopted or took into consideration: (1) people have different needs and are therefore, motivated by different incentives to achieve organisational objectives; and (2) people's needs change predictably over time, meaning that as the needs of people lower in the hierarchy are met, new needs arise. These assumptions led to the recognition that people can be more productive, if unified, despite their diversity which would potentially lead to growth and development for the entire nation.

Another theory that is similar to the framers constitutional consideration was the McGregor's Theory Y. McGregor believed that organisations and institutions that embraced Theory Y were generally more productive. Theory Y adopted a more optimistic view of human nature. Among other things, it theorized that (1) humans can learn to accept and seek responsibilities;

(2) most people possess a high degree of imaginative and problem-solving ability; (3) people will self-govern, or direct themselves toward goals to which they are committed; and, importantly, (4) satisfaction of ego and self-actualisation through the acceptance and respect for diversity.

2. Open System Theory

The term "open systems" reflected the new found belief that all organisations and institutions are unique and should therefore be structured to accommodate the uniqueness and opportunities that the people yawns. In the1960s, it was observed that the traditional bureaucratic feudalistic and colonialistic institutions generally failed to succeed because of the rapid demand for change by the people and the indifference to their cultural diversity. Thus, for an institution or organisation to takeoff, openness in the organisational or institutional structure has to be on solid ground. The Open Systems Theory (OST) integrated in the Nigerian constitution by the framers was an integral phenomenon for the upward mobility of the country. Thus, from the Central and State Government sovereignty, Central and State Governments structures, citizens freedom, rights of citizens, revenue and grants allocations, citizens mobility, judiciary etc. This open system theory (OST) allows for the system to evolve according to the pressure exerted by the various levels of government structures.

The Nigerian constitution open system is embedded with cognitive framework that are consist with morals and behavioral norms that are valued forms of behavioral expectations shared by both the internal and external framework of communities of Nations. Thus, openness in cultures are conspicuous trend that had facilitated expedient interaction among citizens to communicate freely with neighbors and provided stability in the overall process. Through the open system theory (OST), cultures are promulgated in ceremonies, symbols and languages. At ceremonies, cultures commemorate citizens celebrating excellence in life's values. Symbols are visions mission statements that citizen constantly carries or reinforce when representing their Nation or the State. Languages are the exemplification and the spoken identification of the citizens' culture and diversity. As a result, the presence of culture in a system demands uniformity and strength for the nation.

This open system theory (OST) also influences and dictates an institution's or an organisation's growth and development in the economy of the Nation or State. For example, as the overall economy grows the organization or the institution will not only likely to develop but become more specialised. The legal and political system in which an open system operates determines, most importantly, the long-term stability and security of the nation's or organisation's future. In general, the system has to be fair and equitable in all levels of government.

Political Theory of Discentralisation:

As Nigeria became more structured politically, decentralisation became the mainstay of Nigeria political formation. However, advocates of political decentralisation assume that decisions made with greater participation in politics by the citizenry tend to be better informed in diverse society than those made only by the few political authorities in the Central and State Governments. The concept implies that the selection of representatives in congress from local electoral constituencies allows citizens to know their political representatives better and alternatively, allows the representatives to acquaint themselves with the needs and desires of their constituents. The political decentralisation in Nigeria will definitely need an overhaul by the National Electoral Commission (NEC). This statutory reform will be in form of creating democratic simplicity during voting processes and democratic awareness through the media and billboards advertisements to encourage citizens' involvement and to exercise their fundamental rights in the political system.

The political theory of decentralisation enforces the political accountability between politicians approach to federalised government. The more accountable the Central Government is involving with the State Government, the greater the extent of decentralisation. Conversely, in some putative federations, like a Unitary State, decision-making has become so concentrated at the Central Government that the State Governments became a resemblance of administrative extensions of the Central Government rather than autonomous and sovereign Governments. Nigeria being a multi-ethnic country, decentralized federalized institutional arrangements make it possible for her citizens to enjoy the benefits of nationally provided services and a common market while living in relatively homogeneous communities. This kind of self-sorting system allows citizens to make decisions based on considerations of ethnic or linguistic identity as well as economic prospects for the good of all. If citizens place a substantial enough weight on ethnic or linguistic identity, policy preferences from the Central and State Governments are likely to be bound up with deeply felt identities. Therefore, it should be noted that multi-ethnic States may be able to approach the generic incentive problems of decentralisation in a distinctively productive manner.

Some theorists on federalism and decentralisation in both political science and economics spectrum identify numerous advantages in transferring powers and responsibilities to local government. They asserted that ideally, the rewards from each public goods and services attained from a local constituent should fully internalize its benefits and costs. Decentralisation can foster policy innovation and economic growth by stimulating competition among constituents. Decentralisation can also solve credible commitment problems in the protection of property rights and mitigate threats of State predation and civil violence. Decentralisation may also dampen inter-communal tensions in ethnically divided States.

Rational Choice Theories in politics explain why a decentralised system would best satisfy popular preferences in a polity containing heterogeneous individual preferences. Nigerian constitutional theory focuses on the accountability of politicians operating at different levels of government: Presidents, Legislators, and Governors. Several features of the political strata can influence these levels of government. The crucial one is the **Internal Structure of Political Parties**. We begin with the political concerns of Central and State executives. As a result, for the sake of simplicity, Presidents and Governors, and the Legislative interests depends in part on the partisan composition of the government. Under divided government, legislators will be attentive to checking the powers of the President, including the control of resources. If a single party controls both branches of government or the President relies on a majority coalition in the legislature, much will depend on the lines of authority and accountability within the ruling party or parties.

On the other hand, if parties are disciplined and legislators are responsive to the President and National Party leadership or leaderships in the case of coalitions, the outcomes of channel of resources will be tilted towards the President's preferences. However, if legislators are dependent on Governors to advance their political careers, they will naturally seek to curry favor with the Governors including through the design of intergovernmental fiscal relations. Therefore, it should be noted that several features of the political system influences whether lines of authority and accountability within parties legislative preferences. However, it varies in the unitary systems where there are more dependence on States politicians to deliver preferences. As this discussion shows, there is no simple way to measure the extent and nature of fiscal decentralisation.

To find theoretical solutions to this stated problem, genuinely federal institutions must be credibly robust against both Central and State powers. Thus, federal arrangements must represent a commitment by the parties generally to refrain from trespassing on the rights of their political opponents. The obvious way to manage this problem is to enlist independent courts to force both the States and the Central Government to respect jurisdictional boundaries. Alternatively, decentralised practices may be enforced by a system of informal norms that are in place of explicit rules, the various parties should understand and abide with the rules that they are obligated to stay within certain zones of activity, whether or not such zones are enforceable by legal institutions.

Finally, federal promises might be redeemed by a self-enforcing structure of **incentives in** which the elected politicians are bound to stay within their respective zones of action as a matter of political prudence. Such a structure of incentives could in turn support a pattern of practice among the various governments motivated by considerations of power or material interest. For decentralisation to be a credible solution to political problems, it must somehow be supported in one of these three ways. The first two methods involve reliance on a rule of law to enforce decentralised practices, either through explicit rule enforcement or compliance with normative expectations. The last involves the balancing of political opportunities and incentives to stabilize decentralized administration. However, what is particularly significant about Nigerian federalism is that the Framers understood the federal commitment problem and offered both structural and juridical conceptions of federalism as complementary and supplementary solutions.

The founding fathers were certainly clear about the need of a Supreme Court that can play an effective role in enforcing federalism. The Court has both rule of law and institutional incentives to enforce federalism against both Central and State Government when not in compliance of the law. The rule of law incentives derive from the clear instantiation of federalism in the Constitution and from the fact that the stable exercise of political authority in the Nigerian Republic which requires recognition of some degree of local autonomy. The institutional incentives derive from the Court's wish to maintain its role as an arbiter of an evolving federal structure, "an honest broker": if the Court could establish and maintain itself as a neutral broker among the States and between the State and Central Governments, thereto, it assures its own central importance in the governance of a Nation.

The Court has the institutional capacity in accordance to Chapter VII of the constitution of Nigeria, Part 1, and Section 232-236. That is:

232. (1) The Supreme Court shall, to the exclusion of any other court, have original jurisdiction in any dispute between the Federation and a state or between states if and in so far as that dispute involves any question (whether of law or fact) on which the existence or extent of a legal right depends.

(2) In addition to the jurisdiction conferred upon it by subsection (1) of this section, the Supreme Court shall have such original jurisdiction as may be conferred upon it by any Act of the National Assembly.

Provided that no original jurisdiction shall be conferred upon the Supreme Court with respect to any criminal matter.

233. (1) The Supreme Court shall have jurisdiction, to the exclusion of any other court of law in Nigeria, to hear and determine appeals from the Court of Appeal.

(2) An appeal shall lie form decisions of the Court of Appeal to the Supreme Court as of right in the following cases—

(a) where the ground of appeal involves questions of law alone, decisions in any civil or criminal proceedings before the Court of Appeal;

(b) decisions in any civil or criminal proceedings on questions as to the interpretation or application of this constitution,

(c) decisions in any civil or criminal proceedings on questions as to whether any of the provisions of Chapter IV of this Constitution has been, is being or is likely to be, contravened in relation to any person;

(d) decisions in any criminal proceedings in which any person has been sentenced to death by the Court of Appeal or in which the Court of Appeal has affirmed a sentence of death imposed by any other court;

(e) decisions on any question—

(i) whether any person has been validly elected to the office of President or Vice-President under this Constitution,

(ii) whether the term of office of office of President or Vice-President has ceased,

(iii) whether the office of President or Vice-President has become vacant; and

(c) such other cases as may be an Act of the National Assembly.

(3) Subject to the provisions of subsection (2) of this section, an appeal shall lie from the decisions of the Court of Appeal to the Supreme Court with the leave of the Court of Appeal or the Supreme Court.

(4) The Supreme Court may dispose of any application for leave to appeal from any decision of the Court Appeal in respect of any civil or criminal proceedings in the record of the proceedings if the Supreme Court is of opinion that the interests of justice do not require an oral hearing of the application.

(5) Any right of appeal to the supreme Court from the decisions of the Court of Appeal conferred by this section shall be exercisable in the Case of civil proceedings at the instance of a party thereto, or with the leave of the Court of Appeal or the Supreme Court at the instance of an person having an interest in the matter, and in the case of criminal proceedings at the instance of an accused person, or subject to the provisions of this Constitution and any powers conferred upon the Attorney-General of the Federation or the Attorney-General of a state to take over and continue or to discontinue such proceedings, at the instance of such other authorities or persons as may be prescribed.

(6) Any right of appeal to the Supreme Court form the decisions of the Court of Appeal conferred by this section shall, subject to section 236 of this Constitution, be exercised in accordance with any Act of the National Assembly and rules of court for the time being in force regulating the powers, practice and procedure of the Supreme Court.

234. For the purpose of exercising any jurisdiction conferred upon it by this Constitution or any Law, the Supreme Court shall be duly constituted if it consists of not less than five Justices of the Supreme Court:

Provided that where the Supreme Court is sitting to consider an appeal brought under 233(2)(b) or (c) of this Constitution, or to exercise its original jurisdiction in accordance with section 232 of this Constitution, the Court shall be constituted by seven Justices.

235. Without prejudice to the powers of the President or of the Governor of a state with respect to prerogative of mercy, no appeal shall lie to any other body or person from any determination of the Supreme Court.

236. Subject to the provisions of any Act of the National Assembly, the Chief Justice of Nigeria may make rules for regulating the practice and procedure of the Supreme Court."

Fiscal and Decentralised Theory of Nigerian Federalism:

Fiscal federalism is the concept that constitutes sets of guiding principles, guiding concept from the constitution that helps in designing financial relations between the Central and State Governments. On the other hand, fiscal decentralisation is a process of applying such principles to all levels of government. The Fiscal federalism principles guide how boundaries, assignments, the levels and nature of transfers should be revised to ensure efficiency and perhaps equity. Thus, fiscal federalism provides the tools for application of the federal approach to governance. The complementary roles of the Central and State Governments are determined by analyzing the most effective ways and means of achieving a desired objective. Federalism in Nigeria is characterized by constitutional demarcation of revenue and expenditure powers among the levels of government.

The Constitution also requires the President upon the receipt of advice from the Revenue Mobilisation Allocation and Fiscal Commission, to table before the National Assembly proposals for revenue allocation from the Federation Account, and in determining the formula, the National Assembly will take into account, the allocation principles especially those of population equality of States, internal revenue generation, land mass terrain as well as population density; provided that the principle of derivation is constantly reflected in any approved formula. Each of the

State Governments has devolved powers to levy certain taxes to the various communities in their local areas.

The States have also instituted a system of sharing of States' revenues to local bodies. The amount standing to the credit of Local Government Councils in the Federation Account will be allocated to the State for the benefit of their Local Government Councils on such terms and in such manner as may be prescribed by the National Assembly. Each State will maintain a special account to be called "State Joint Local Government Account" into which all allocations to the Local Government will be paid. Each State shall pay to Local Government Councils in its area of jurisdiction such proportion of its total revenue on such terms and in such manner as may be prescribed by the National Assembly.

An important observation that can be precondition for the efficient functioning of a multi-level fiscal system is to have a proper assignment system. Some of the most important feature of a proper assignment system are: (i) the functionality and sources of finance should be based on comparative advantage; (ii) revenue powers should be aligned to the assignment of expenditure functions; (iii) State Governments should not have powers to undo the national initiative on stabilisation and redistribution; (iv) a proper mechanism should be instituted to deal with vertical and horizontal overlapping of tax and disbursement systems and (v) there should a mechanism to offset the fiscal disabilities through a system of well designed intergovernmental transfers.

The functions related to money supply, external borrowing, international relations, defense, energy, space, national highways, airways, international waterways, and those having significant economies of scale are assigned exclusively to the Central Government. Furthermore, the functions involving benefits spanning across States and matters with significant developmental potential are undertaken concurrently with the States. These include economic planning, energy, education, health and family welfare. Notably, the tax powers are assigned on the basis of the principle of separation and are assigned exclusively either to the Central or the States. However, the separation is only in legal and not in economic sense. Thus, the central can levy taxes on production (excise duty); whereas, the tax on sale or purchase of goods has to be levied by the States. Similarly, only the States can levy the taxes on agricultural incomes and businesses and the Central Government can levy taxes on non-agricultural incomes and natural resources.

According to the federal constitution of Nigeria, Chapter VI, the Executive, Part C, Section 162(2-10) explained the central government of Nigeria distributive funds as it relates to fiscal federalism:

"162 (2) The President, upon the receipt of advice from the Revenue Mobilisation Allocation and Fiscal Commission, shall table before the National Assembly proposals for revenue allocation from the Federation Account, and in determining the formula, the National Assembly shall take into account, the allocation principles especially those of population, equality of States, internal revenue generation, land mass, terrain as well as population density;

Provided that the principle of derivation shall be constantly reflected in any approved formula as being not less than thirteen per cent of the revenue accruing to the Federation Account directly from any natural resources.

(3) Any amount standing to the credit of the Federation Account shall be distributed among the Federal and State Governments and the Local Government Councils in each State on such terms and in such manner as may be prescribed by the National Assembly.

(4) Any amount standing to the credit of the States in the Federation Account shall be distributed among the States on such terms and in such manner as may be prescribed by the National Assembly.

(5) The amount standing to the credit of Local Government Councils in the Federation Account shall also be allocated to the State for the benefit of their Local Government Councils on such terms and in such manner as may be prescribed by the National Assembly.

(6) Each State shall maintain a special account to be called "State Joint Local Government Account" into which shall be paid all allocations to the Local Government Councils of the State from the Federation Account and from the Government of the State.

(7) Each State shall pay to Local Government Councils in its area of jurisdiction such proportion of its total revenue on such terms and in such manner as may be prescribed by the National Assembly.

(8) The amount standing to the credit of Local Government Councils of a State shall be distributed among the Local Government Councils of that State on such terms and in such manner as may be prescribed by the House of Assembly of the State.

(9) Any amount standing to the credit of the judiciary in the Federation Account shall be paid directly to the National Judicial Councils for disbursement to the heads of courts established for the Federation and the States under section 6 of this Constitution.

(10) For the purpose of subsection (1) of this section, "revenue" means any income or return accruing to or derived by the Government of the Federation from any source. The President, upon the receipt of advice from the Revenue Mobilisation Allocation and Fiscal Commission, shall table before the National Assembly proposals for revenue allocation from the Federation Account, and in determining the formula, the National Assembly shall take into account, the allocation principles especially those of population, equality of States, internal revenue generation, land mass, terrain as well as population density."

The Central sector schemes are entirely funded by the Central Government and the States are merely implementing agencies. The centrally sponsored schemes are shared cost programs requiring, the States to make matching contributions. Assignment between State and Local Government revenue and expenditure assignments in the lists are concurrent with the States' responsibilities and the actual assignment of specific revenue sources and expenditure depends on the extent to which the State is willing to devolve. The extent of devolution of powers and functions to Local Governments show wide variation depending on the willingness of the State Government to devolve functions and powers to the Local Governments.

The State Government passes on the funds for implementation of various central sector and centrally sponsored schemes to the Local Governments. The most important of them is for poverty alleviation, but there are also other schemes on social and community services in which the local governments have a comparative advantage in implementation. From observation, it shows that Local Governments have very little flexibility in the use of funds. After deductions of charges for electricity and other facilities by State Government in the general purpose transfers, very little is left. A bulk of what is available is needed for administration and the Local Governments are hardly in a position to execute any developmental schemes.

In decentralisation, the policy makers purportedly envisaged the panacea of many ills afflicting the society. It is expected to achieve many things such as enable efficient allocation of resources, improve governance, accelerate economic growth, reduce poverty, achieve a gender balance and empower weaker sections of society. Decentralisation will necessarily result in more efficient delivery of public services irrespective of the capacity of the institutions and economic setting.

This enthusiasm is seen in Nigeria with federal constitution that focused on the democratisation of polity that addresses the multi-party system, transition to a market economy, and accommodating the diverse ethnic, linguistic identities and diversities. However, the Nigeria experiences underline the fact that there is much to be done to create appropriate conditions for fiscal decentralization to be successful in achieving her objectives. According to Tanzi (1996), federalist fiscal system where States functions and sources of finance are clearly defined according to the constitution and the Local Governments are required to strictly manage their expenditures from within their means, decentralisation does not pose serious problems for macroeconomic management.

The experience of decentralisation in Nigeria should help us to gain better understanding of the preconditions and institutional requirements and capacity development necessary for fiscal decentralisation to achieve efficient and equitable delivery of public services. The Nigeria federalism framework experience was not congenial for the development of local self-government in most of the States. The oligopolistic power structure in local jurisdictions did not provide the elected members a representative character. The socially disadvantaged groups who also belonged to poorer sections of society did not effectively participate in the decentralization process. There was no mechanism to prevent the State Governments from superseding the duly elected Local Governments.

The fiscal powers of the Local Governments did not generate adequate revenues and they had to perennially depend upon the State Government grants for providing services for projects in the local communities. Another issue of the fiscal discentralisation is the Central Government inabilities to control its own deficits as a result impose hard budget constraint on the States. Despite the Central Government fiscal inadequacies and the powers to control in the structural deficits of States' fiscal operations, the States have found a variety of ways to overcome their hard budget constraint. In other words, the fiscal system and arrangements have not been able to prevent the States from indulging in fiscal profligacy. Disincentives to fiscal prudence in the transfer system, the irrelevant distinction between planned and non-planned expenditures, growing populism associated with coalition politics, the culture of free-riding are some of the major factors responsible.

The resulting vertical and horizontal fiscal imbalances have to be offset through a system of unconditional intergovernmental transfers. It is generally recognised that (i) the transfer system should be formula based rather than negotiated; (ii) the design of transfers should not have adverse incentives in fiscal management, in particular, general purpose transfers should be designed to offset shortfall in revenue capacity and excess expenditure needs of States; and (iii) specific purpose transfers should be designed to ensure minimum standards of targeted services.

The Nigerian constitution makes an implicit assumption that the assignment system results in surpluses for the Central Government and therefore, provides for transfers to States by way of tax devolution and grants in aid of revenues. To determine the transfers the constitution provides for the institution Revenue Mobilisation Allocation and Fiscal Commission. The Commission is required to recommend derivation of taxes from the Central Government to the State Governments and provide grants to the States in need of additional assistance.

The Polity and Policy of Nigerian Federation System

Federalism has been purported to be practiced in Nigeria since Nigeria became known as a country. However, since the inception of the constitution, most Nigerians has contrasted federalism with unitary system of governance in Nigeria. Thus, as aforementioned in chapter one, under the unitary system, there may be only one level of government or the States are subordinate to the Central Government and the Central Government can implement policies without States inputs and institute orders to the States or the Local Government for compliance. However, in contrast, the Nigerian Central Government cannot order any State Governments under the present civilian democratic government to implement orders in their States that they are not obligated to perform. State governments have powers and sovereignty to implement laws pertaining to the welfare of their states and are not answerable to the Central Government. The Central and the State Governments are separately answerable to the citizens of their various constituents. Some of the important features of federalism in Nigeria are:

1. There are two or more levels or tiers of government. The different levels of government govern the same constituents. Each level has their own jurisdiction in some specific matters of legislation, taxation and administration.
2. The constitution specifically states the jurisdictions of the respective levels or tiers of government and their existence and authority are fully guaranteed.

3. The fundamental provisions of the constitution cannot be unilaterally changed by one level of government. Such changes require the consent of both the levels of government for rectification.

4. The judicial branch of government has the power to interpret the constitution and the powers of different levels of government. The Supreme Court interprets the disputes in law if arise between the different levels of governments.

5. There is revenue autonomy for each levels of government as clearly specified in the constitution.

6. In the federal system of Nigeria, governments at different levels agree to some rules of power sharing. The Central Government is obligated to promote unity and accommodate diversity among the states.

In Nigeria, the federal constitution promulgated a balance of power that is trusted and respected by the levels of governments and had foster an ideal federalism system for governing the country. This balance depends mainly on the historical context in which the federation was formed.

How Federalism is Practiced in Nigeria:

The successful noted practice of federalism in Nigeria is virtually due to the enacted constitution. However, it can be argued that the constitutional provisions are not necessarily the only success of federalism; but, the attributes of the nature of democratic politics in the country. Such as, the diversity of shared ideals, respect for culture and arts, and language diversity.

Culture and Arts:

The acceptance and celebration of Nigeria arts and cultures was the first and major test for democratic politics in the country. This diversity had assisted in creating many more States from the Nigeria original three provisional regions established in the 1960 constitution. This creation of new States was instituted to ensure that citizens' who spoke the same language and observed the same art and culture, geographical attributes, and ethnicity will live in the same State. Even though, some national leaders in Nigeria oppose the creation of more States on the premise of diversity, they argued that it will possibly lead to the disintegration of the country. The Central Government and National assembly resisted on the diversity, ethnicity, and language as factors of the formation and retention of unity.

Language:

A second attributes of the nature of democratic politics in Nigeria is the language policy. The Nigerian constitution did not give the status of national language to any one language ethnic group. There are about 280 languages with three (Ibo, Yoruba, and Hausa) identified major languages or scheduled Languages by the constitution. The framers adopted a very cautious attitude in choosing any of the major languages as the National language for the country. Thus, according to the constitution, the use of English along with the three major languages to continues to be the official policy languages of the Government of Nigeria. Despite, there is flexibility in the use of other remaining 280 languages across Nigeria.

One other way federalism has shown success is the formation of the Central and State relations. The constitution enforced the separation of powers between the executive branches despite the differences of their political parties. This means that the State governments with different political party affiliation can exercise their rights as autonomous and sovereign from the ruling federal government with different political party affiliation. This phenomenon spirit of federalism enacted in the constitution has brought unification among diverse groups of people with scattered cultures and languages. This system produces a progressive reduction of cultural and regional tensions and differences and created a homogenous political system that apparently has the means of economic and social resolution processes without resort to large-scale physical force among the units of governments.

However, the bottom line is to provide process for peaceful transitional change the desired natural outcome of citizens' relations. Nigeria is known for her pluralistic and segmented secular society. In practice of the federal system and for the implementation of a workable democracy, the system has to employ a form of quota in education, federal and state employment, and zoning in political appointments. This application was measured to protect the minority from the majority and to avoid or reduce the trends of nepotism in the configurations of the Nigerian polity.

Nigeria federalists challenge is the cohesiveness of apprehension of the true nature of the commitment and practice of federalism and democracy. The Central Government should know how to reconcile the dispensation of political powers in a meaningful sense of ethnic identity without compromising the essence of democracy with a quota syndrome that encourages entitlements and inefficiencies in government. The purpose is to accommodate and encourage cultural diversity, and uphold an effective democracy that eliminate quota of any kind and also abide and respect the constitution without any national political interference. However, granted that events do have its intrinsic consequences when foundation of any structure is being tinkered with. As in the case of the federal constitution, by observation, the Nigerian Central and State Governments negates the compliance of the separation of religion and state in the constitution, thereby, in most cases allowed religion to interfere with the affairs of state.

Central and State Governments Relationships in a Federalised System of Nigeria:

Since the signing of the federated Nigerian Constitution, the division of power in Nigeria has been based on sharing power between the Central and State Government s. The Nigerian power distribution is shown in the underline table below.

Table 1.1: Nigerian Power Distribution

Central Government	State Government
• Paper/Coin money. • Declare war. • Conduct foreign relations. • Oversee foreign and interstate trade.	• Ratify amendments. • Manage public health and safety. • Oversee trade within the state.

In addition, the Central and State Governments share the following powers:

• Make and enforce laws
• Taxes
• Borrow money;
• Manage Public health and safety.

It should be noteworthy to indicate that the policies as enacted in the constitution do not protect the sovereignty of State Governments. The constitution divides authority between Federal and State Governments for the protection of all citizens irrespective of their State of origins. State sovereignty is not just an end in itself, but a means for the protection and the attainable welfare of all her citizens. In all, federalism secures all citizens, the liberties that derive from the diffusion of sovereign power. Federal polity is the key elements of debates and discussions about democratisation, decentralisation, individual rights protection, and minority community guarantees.

The Nigerian Federalism policies are observed as being successful and the Nigerian democratic mode of governance is extraordinarily careful. In the same token, it is observed that her democratic modes of governance can be maintained for centuries if she continued to persist and maintain the set ideologies of the framers original constitutional framework. The framers reflected in their ideas the policies and principles of necessity and desirability of federalism rather than unitary approach. The necessity and desirability of federalism lies in the need to develop modes of intra and inter-government governance for the benefit of unity in a diverse demographic society that is expected to function progressively beyond competent expectations in a complicated political environment. Insofar, such functional diversity has a territorial scope of racial, ethnic, religious, linguistic and nationality commitments that seek to retain these identities for a progressive federalism and a better, enviable Nigeria.

The intent of the framers of the constitution was believed to have created a covenant between the levels of government for the purpose of retaining identity and integrity through political entities that will better serve the citizens they duly represent. As such, covenant in the framers view signifies a binding partnership among co-equals levels of governments in a binding commitment to partner with each other in the spirit of the law rather than merely the letter of the law. The Nigerian framers also invoked covenant in federalism polity as a mode to commit the various parties in government to endure and promote a perpetual relationship of cooperation in achieving peaceful resolve to conflicts and diversity.

In Nigeria policy, the framers enacted federalism in the constitution as both a structure and a process of governance that establishes unity on the basis of consent while preserving diversity and identities by constitutionally uniting separate political communities into a progressive body. In Nigeria policy, powers, are divided and shared between the Central and State Governments. This division of powers is combined with authoritative capacity to carry out those responsibilities on behalf of the citizens of the Federation and of the States. The distribution of powers is also intended to protect both the integral authorities of the constituent governments, as well as, the perpetual integrity of their respective communities.

The Nigeria democratic federation policy is to foster cooperation for peace and security, the construct of common good, migration and communication of liberty, the moderation of citizens diversity, guarding against centralized tyranny by either the minority or the majority of the population. This policy also promote vibrant common market, citizens participation in political affairs from the Central, State, and Local Government levels, access to innovation and invention capabilities, promoting government efficiencies in public recreations and services. It also, facilitates the process of justice by matching the benefits of government closely to the burdens of paying for government, such as taxes. Though, the process of policy and polity in government can be very complex and complicated which foster unevenness in development in various jurisdictions that may subsequently affect inherent inequality and subject to paralysis in decision-making process in the system.

The orbiter of the Nigerian federalism lies on the power of the Constituent States and the Presidential System of governance. The umpire of the federal system is the Supreme Court that has the power of resolving inter-governmental and jurisdictional conflicts. However, citizen participation and rule of public transparency are the fundamental characteristics of the success to a federal system. As observed in the Nigerian Constitution intra and inter-governmental cooperation are crucial in solving public problems especially when pragmatic approach is being used as a policy to deal with the citizens issues. Thus, federal loyalty is an essential factor in calibrating moral commitment in the system to achieve the objectives and goals of a progressive federal government. In moving forward, the federal polity and policy should have the willingness to compromise, exercise the fortitude of forbearance, and the wisdom to listen for another citizen point of views.

The derivation policy as described in the Nigerian Constitution that the federal government should engage in inter-governmental transfers; whereby, these transfers desire the Central Government to maintain partnership with the State Governments by decentralizing revenue expenditures and centralizing revenue. The Central Government also engages in fiscal equalization through grants to State Governments in shortfalls in order to lift the States fiscal capacity for service provisions. However, each government, as a policy, has sufficient autonomous legislative capacity, administrative and fiscal know-how, to perform their required duties to their constituents without totally dependent or subservient to the Central Government. Historically, the allocation of revenues has been highly contentious between the Central Government and State Governments' when the shared derivation is outside the constitutional mandate. Thus, the polity of democratic accountability in taxing and spending had played a tremendous impact on revenue allocation policy. Constituent States that experiences the extraction of more revenues from their States(large mineral States) to the Federal coffers were rewarded with more revenue allocation based on the derivation shared policy.

Nigeria being a multi-cultural and ethnically diverse state has been steadily glued together with aid of the constitutional framework that accommodated the policy of racial, ethnic, religious, and linguistic phenomenon into a single polity. it is also evident that federal accommodations of these diversity has been quite a difficult and delicate achievements. For instance, certain disserting groups in Nigeria federation that are expressing support for devolution or decentralization, argued assiduously against federalism. Although, such resistance to federalism can itself is a subterfuge for resisting democratization, which may otherwise possibility lead to disintegration of a Nation.

The upholding of the constitution in all its true meaning in shaping public policies of the land is a conception of national unity. Federalism as a polycentric is neither non-centralized nor domineering system of governance and should be viewed neither by the Central nor the State Governments' elites as a tool to unilaterally forestall or alter the constitutional distribution of policy and polity to fit their selfish needs. Hitherto, federalism as enacted by the framers of the constitution which is a covenant between equal levels of governments with respect to freedom, equity, and diversity of all citizens should be the only functional authority for policy enactment in the federation.

Taxonomy

A *federal political order*: Is taken to be "the genus of political organization that is marked by the combination of shared rule and self-rule" (Watts 1998, 120). *Federalism* is the theory or advocacy of such an order, including principles for dividing final authority between member units and the common institutions. Federal political orders are typically arranged to constrain the central government and prevent majorities from overriding a state governments.

A *federation:* Is one species of such a federal order; other species are unions, confederations, leagues and decentralised unions. A *federation* in this sense involves a *territorial* division of power between constituent units—called 'state governments. This division of power is typically entrenched in a constitution which neither a member unit nor the state government can alter unilaterally. The central government and the state governments have direct effect on the citizenry and the representatives of governments are directly elected. In contrast, 'confederation' has come to mean a political order with a weaker center than a federation. Typically, in a confederation, a state government may legally exit; the central government only exercises authority delegated by the state government; the central government is subject to state government veto on many issues; central government decisions bind state governments but not citizens directly; the central government lacks an independent fiscal or electoral base; the state governments do not cede authority permanently to the central government. Confederations are often based on agreements for specific tasks, and the central government may be completely exercised by delegates of the state governments. Federations can involve state governments in central decision-making in at least two different ways: State government representatives participate in the administration of the central government—in cabinets and in the collective legislative arrangements.

Conclusion

In this book, we have tried to understand the Nigeria federal system and its basic peculiarities and inherited problems. This analytical examination has revealed that stability or instability of the polarization society of Nigeria has been managed with a functional federalism. The federal system had held a better prospect in helping to stem a major source of political instability in Nigerian. Although, this unified system, is not without its' follies in implementation due to the leadership approach; but the Nigerian political environment has demonstrated that federal system is workable tool in a democratic system of government.

The Nigerian federal structure had seemingly succeeded in solving and stabilizing the political mishaps between functional parties. As indicated in the text, leadership approach and the fundamental principles of integrity and authenticity, open policy, and respect for diversity as designed in the constitution by the framers are the functional principles that will catapult the vision of the country to an equitable and developed state.

Soothing efforts should be diverted to the future generations of leadership that will instill a directed leadership policy that would inspire citizens especially youths to be more diverse in their thinking vis a vis innovation and invention possibilities that are geared towards nation building and the philosophy of selflessness. Further citizens exposure on government functionality and accountability and the various governmental enlightenment schemes like encouraging frequent voting and citizens participation will assist in promoting positive and learning process needed in providing trust that is lacking in the federalism as a system of governance.

Our framers had laid the foundation and the structure of democracy for all her citizens, therefore, it is absolutely necessary for the present generation to pass a "clean bill of trust and integrity" in leadership and the protection of the constitutional framework enacted by the founding fathers of Nigeria to the future generation. Thus, according to Gambari (2008), nations just don't happen by historical accident; rather they are built by exemplary men and women with vision and resolve and sustained by institutions that promote good governance in all levels of the Nigeria constituents.

References

Abia, B. E. (2006). Understanding Nigerian Government and Politics 2nd ed. Lagos, Gofaflesh Publications.

Acton, L. and Figgis, J. N. (1907). "Nationality," (ed.). *The History of Freedom and Other Essays*, London: Macmillan.

Anderson, G. (2007). Nigerian Fiscal Federalism Seen from a Comparative Perspective. October. Notes for Address to Governors' Forum, Abuja, Nigeria.

Bauer, O. (2000). *The Question of Nationalities and Social Democracy*. Minneapolis: University of Minnesota Press.

Beer, S. H., (1993). *To Make a Nation: the Rediscovery of American Federalism*, Cambridge, MA: Harvard University Press.

Bednar, J., Eskridge, W.N., Ferejohn, J. (1999). A Political Theory of Federalism. Encyclopedia of Business. 2nd ed.,

Blankart, C. B. (2000). The Process of Government Centralization: A Constitutional View," Constitutional Political Economy, 11, March, 27-39.

Bowman, A.O. (2004). Horizontal Federalism: Exploring Interstate Interactions. Journal of Public Administration Research and Theory. 14

Braybrooke, D. (1983). "Can Democracy Be Combined With Federalism or With Liberalism?", in J. R. Pennock and John W. Chapman (eds.), *Nomos XXV: Liberal Democracy*, New York, London: New York University Press.

Buchanan, J. (1995). "Federalism as an ideal political order and an objective for constitutional reform," *Publius*. 25(2): 19-27.

Buchanan, J.M. (1995/96). "Federalism and Individual Sovereignty." Cato Journal. 15: 264-65.

Bulama, J.B. Federalism and the Nigeria experience: A sword or a shield? Law school, University of Jos. Nigeria.

Carens, J. H. (2000). *Culture, Citizenship, and Community. A Contextual Exploration of Justice as Evenhandedness.* Oxford: Oxford University Press.

Choudhry, S. (2001). "Citizenship and Federations: Some Preliminary Reflections," in Nicolaidis and Howse (eds.) 377-402.

Constitution of the Federal Republic of Nigeria. (1999) "Amended" Internation Center for Nigerian Law.

Ebula, R.J. (1979). *The Determinants of Human Migration,* Lexington: Lexington Book.

Enahoro, A. (1997). The 5th Yoruba National Convention held at Houston, TexasS, USA Saturday, 26th April.

Federalism and Development in Nigeria. Shara Reporters, Posted: April 16, 2010.

Filippov, M., Peter, C.O., and Olga, S. (2003). *Designing Federalism: A Theory of Self-Sustainable Federal Institutions,* Cambridge: Cambridge University Press.

Frey, B.S. and Alois, S. (2000). "Happiness Prospers in Democracy," *Journal of Happiness Studies,* 1(1):79-102.

Gagnon, A.G., and James, T. (eds.) (2001). *Multinational Democracies,* Cambridge: Cambridge University Press.

Garman, C., Stephan H., Eliza,W. (2001). Fiscal Decentralization: A Political Theory with Latin American Cases. World Politics. Publisher: JSTOR. 53(2): 205-236.

Gerber, E.R. (1999). *The Populist Paradox,* Princeton: Princeton University Press.

Grossman, P. J. and Edwin, G. W. (1994). "Federalism and the Growth of Government Revisited," *Public Choice,* April. 79:19-32.

Grubb, W.N. (1982). "The Dynamic Implications of the Tiebout Model—the Changing Composition of Boston Communities, 1960-1970," *Public Finance Quarterly.* 10:17-38.

Gutmann, A. (ed.), (1994). *Multiculturalism: Examining the Politics of Recognition,* Princeton: Princeton University Press.

Infortainment (1999-2010).Constitution of the Federal Republic of Nigeria. International Center for Nigeria law.

Karmis, D. and Wayne N. (eds.), (2005). *Theories of Federalism: A Reader*, New York: Palgrave.

Knop, K. et al (eds.) (1995). *Rethinking Federalism: Citizens, Markets and Governments in a Changing World*. Vancouver: University of British Columbia Press.

Kymlicka, W., and Wayne N. (eds.) (2000). *Citizenship in Diverse Societies*. Oxford: Oxford University Press.

Litvack, J., Junaid A., and Richard B. (1998). "Rethinking Decentralization at the World Bank". Sector Studies Series. The World Bank.

Muhammed, A. A. (2007). Reflections on Five Decades of Nigerian Federalism. Jimoh, H. I. et al (eds.), Perspectives on Nation Building.

Natufe, O, I. et al. Federalism in Nigeria. Okpe Union of North America. June 22, 2005.

Nicolaidis, K. and Robert H. (eds.), (2001). *The Federal Vision: Legitimacy and Levels of Governance in the US and the EU*. Oxford: Oxford University Press.

Nnamdi, H. S. (2009). Nigerian Government and Politics: Trust Publications, Lagos, Nigeria.

Oates, W.E. (1999). "An Essay on Fiscal Federalism" *Journal of Economic Literature*. Vol. No. XXXVII. 3: 1120-1149.

Okoeki, O. (2009). Quest for true Federalism in Nigeria.

Osifeso, I. (2010) Nigeria Federalism and Devoluyion. November 26. Iiishan-Remo, Ogun State, Nigeria.

Rao, G.M. (1998), "Intergovernmental Fiscal relations in a Planned Economy: The case of India" in Richard Bird and Francois Vaillancourt (Eds), *Fiscal Decentralization in Developing Countries*, Cambridge University Press. 78-114.

Rao, G.M. and Tapas K. S. (1996), *Fiscal Federalism in India—Theory and Practice*, Macmillan India, New Delhi.

Rao, G.M. (1998). Fiscal Decentralisation in Indian Federalism. Institute of Social and economic Change. Bangalore, India.

Rodden, J. (2003). "Reviving Leviathan: Fiscal Federalism and the Growth of Government." *International Organization.* Fall. (57):695-729.

Rodden, J. and Erik, W. (2002). "Beyond the Fiction of Federalism," *World Politics, July.* (54):494-531.

Levy, J. (2004). "National Minorities Without Nationalism," in Alain Dieckhoff (ed.), *The Politics of Belonging: Nationalism, Liberalism, and Pluralism,* Lanham, MD: Rowman & Littlefield.

Levy, J. (2007). "Federalism and the Old and New Liberalisms," *Social Philosophy and Policy,* 24(1):306-26.

Levy, J. (2008). "Self-determination, non-domination, and federalism," *Hypatia,* 23(3): 60-78.

Sagay, I. Nigeria: Federalism, the constitution and resource control. Text of speech deliveredat the fourth sensitisation programme organised by the Ibori Vanguard at the Lagoon Restaurant, Lagos.

Tanzi, V. (1996), "Fiscal Federalism and Decentralization: A Review of Some Efficiency and Macroeconomic Aspects", Annual Bank Conference on Development Economics, May 1-2, Washington DC

Trechsel, A. (ed.) (2006). *Towards a Federal Europe.* London: Routledge.

Tushnet, M. (ed.) (1990). *Comparative Constitutional Federalism: Europe and America,* New York: Greenwood Press.

Wisdom, I. et al. (2011). Federalism in Nigeria: Problem and Prospects of consolidation. A Seminar Paper presented in the Department of Political Science and Public Administration, University of Benin, Benin City, Nigeria.

Profile

Name in Full:	Sunday Christopher Enubuzor, Ph.D.
Post Desired	Professor
Place of Birth	Lagos, Nigeria
Nationality	Nigeria/United States (Dual Citizen)
Marital Status	Married
Number of Age of Children	13, 14, 19, 25, and 29
Home and Postal Address	6421 Ranchview Lane, N; Maple Grove, MN 55311. USA
E-mail Address:	*senubuzor@yahoo.com*
Telephone Numbers	763-355-5513—Home; 763-868-6671—Cell

Educational Institutions Attended	1. B.A State University of New York College @ Cortland, New York; August 1983 to June 1987.
	2. M.S New York Institute of Technology, Old Westbury, New York. February 1991 to June 1992.
	3. Ph.D. Walden University, Minneapolis, Minnesota September 2007 to June 2011.
Last Diploma Held	Doctor of Philosophy in Applied Management and Decision Sciences; Specialization: Leadership and Organizational Change. June 2011.
Previous Employers	1. Nigerian Police Force; **Position Held:** Inspector; **Dates:** 1978-1983.
	2. Marine Midland Bank, New York; **Position Held:** Credit Analyst; **Dates:** 1987-1990.
	3. Harrisun Energy Associates; **Position Held:** Energy Consultant; **Dates:** 1992-2000.
	4. US Airways; **Position Held:** Supervisor; **Dates:** 2000-2003.
2.	
Recent Employers:	5. Harrsun Enterprises, LLP; **Position Held:** President/CEO. **Dates:** 2003-2009.
	6. DeVry University and Kelly Graduate School; **Position Held:** Contract Professor; **Dates:** 2010-Present.
Interest	Soccer, Golf, and Tennis (Lawn and Table)

Award:	Honor Society SIGMA IOTA EPSILON, ZETA RHO CHAPTER, Walden University, School of Management.
Distinction and Publication:	Dissertation peer-reviewed published by ProQuest.
	Socioeconomic Stratification: A Case Study on Sustainable Growth in a Declining Population. Xlibris Publishing
	The Practice of Nigerian Federalism Xlibris Publishing

www.ingramcontent.com/pod-product-compliance
Lightning Source LLC
Chambersburg PA
CBHW031249280526
45784CB00004B/1776